INSIDE THE DEATH CHAMBER

INSIDE THE DEATH CHAMBER

Exploring Executions

L. KAY GILLESPIE

Weber State University

Boston ■ New York ■ San Francisco
Mexico City ■ Montreal ■ Toronto ■ London ■ Madrid ■ Munich ■ Paris
Hong Kong ■ Singapore ■ Tokyo ■ Cape Town ■ Sydney

Series Editor: *Jennifer Jacobson*
Editorial Assistant: *Elizabeth Lee*
Executive Marketing Manager: *Brad Parkins*
Editorial-Production Service: *Omegatype Typography, Inc.*
Composition Buyer: *Linda Cox*
Manufacturing Buyer: *Andrew Turso*
Cover Administrator: *Kristina Mose-Libon*
Electronic Composition: *Omegatype Typography, Inc.*

For related titles and support materials, visit our online catalog at www.ablongman.com.

Library of Congress Cataloging-in-Publication Data

Gillespie, L. Kay.
    Inside the death chamber: exploring executions / L. Kay Gillespie.
       p. cm.
    Includes bibliographical references and index.
    ISBN 0-205-35257-X
       1. Capital punishment—United States. 2. Executions and executioners—United States.
3. Death row inmates—United States. 4. Punishment—United States—Philosophy. 5.
Lethal injection (Execution)—Moral and ethical aspects—United States. I. Title.

HV8699.U5 G54 2003
364.66'0973—dc21

                                           2002025550

Dedicated to Marilynn and the kids—for their sacrifices

CONTENTS

CHAPTER THREE
Process Questions   35

FOREWORD

It may be hard to believe that Americans in the 1950s and early 1960s were overwhelmingly *against* the death penalty. During this period in our history, the crime rate was still low enough to keep most people from fearing they would be brutally slain by a cold-blooded killer. Few people were filled with anxiety about possibly being victimized by sexual predators, serial killers, mass murderers, or the like. They saw no need to kill in order to avoid being killed.

By the mid-1960s, however, all of that had changed, as the gigantic baby-boomer cohort reached its "crime-prone" teenage years and the rate of serious crime including murder began to soar. Through the 1970s, as the crime rate continued its ascent, more and more Americans, feeling increasingly vulnerable, were demanding loudly that the criminal justice system be toughened to protect them from evil. As an aspect of this new preference for law and order, widespread opposition to capital punishment soon evaporated and was replaced with pervasive support for executing convicted killers.

Reflecting an unexpected increase in the murder rate beginning in the mid-1980s, support for the death penalty has continued into the new millennium. In a recent Gallup survey (May 20, 2002), 72 percent of all Americans reported being in favor of capital punishment; only 25 percent voiced their opposition. Yet a sizable segment of the population apparently also recognizes problems with administering the death penalty. When given the sentencing alternative of life without parole eligibility, almost half of those surveyed favored life imprisonment. Moreover, much of the support for capital punishment is qualified support: 82 percent oppose the death penalty for people with mental retardation, 73 percent oppose it for those with mental illnesses, and 69 percent oppose the death penalty for juvenile offenders.

I haven't taken a survey, but I would bet that most criminologists disagree with the majority of Americans about the effectiveness of executing defendants who commit murder. The literature of criminology is filled with studies that conclude that the death penalty simply does not work—it doesn't appear to deter other individuals from committing murder and might even encourage a copycat phenomenon; it costs far more to administer than placing a defendant behind bars for forty years; and it is often applied in an uneven and discriminatory way. Most damning of all, scores of innocent people have been exonerated only after they were executed by the state.

The author of *Inside the Death Chamber* is not altogether impressed with the objective and quantitative research, nor does he reject it. Unlike many other criminologists, he takes a position in the middle of the controversy, being unwilling to join the ranks of either the death penalty fanatics or the anti–death penalty zealots. Unlike many other criminologists, Professor Gillespie goes beyond what can be objectively studied. Drawing on a wealth of professional as well as personal experience, he examines both the subjective and objective evidence to explore executions as they have never before been explored. And along the way, acting as a social scientist as well as a human being, he uncovers many hidden complexities in the debate and provides a fascinating overview of capital punishment from which students will learn a great deal.

Professor Gillespie never insults students—he merely challenges them to go beyond the oversimplified arguments they have heard elsewhere. His book will help students understand the wide range of factors to be considered in taking an informed and compassionate position about one of the most important criminal justice issues facing our nation.

Jack Levin, Director
The Brudnick Center on Violence and Conflict
Northeastern University

PREFACE

The question I am most frequently asked about my research on capital punishment is, "Why don't they just shoot the bastards?" The most practical question I am asked is, "What do you wear to an execution?" Both are rhetorical questions. Although the first question may appear crass and somewhat ignorant, it reflects much of the public's attitude about the death penalty. These serious offenders whom we sentence to death are perceived as "bastards," "beasts," and as part of the ever-present flotsam and jetsam of our modern society. The fact that many of them are someone's fathers and mothers and even someone's children gets lost in the thirst for societal revenge. The practical question reflects a curiosity about how one prepares to witness or participate in an execution. I have done both.

While visiting what remains of the boys' prison at Point Puer on the island of Tasmania, I discovered a clay brick used in the construction of the cell houses that incarcerated prisoners transported from England to Australia. The archeologist I was with explained to me that, as the boys made these bricks, they would press their thumb into the corner of each brick before it was fired, signifying that they did, in fact, exist—even though separated from everything and everyone they knew in England.

It is the firsthand knowledge of the meaning of this existence, even that of those who live on death row, that drives my research interest. Too easily people become numbers and objects. Researchers maintain their distance from the people they study and, too often, these people then become "subjects" and statistics.

With regard to the death penalty, we know how many have been executed, what methods have been used, and how many await execution on death rows across the nation. However, we do not know whom we execute, what the death row experience is about, and how they meet their deaths. Wherever I go there is a great curiosity, sometimes morbid, about the execution process. People are attracted, yet repulsed, by this ultimate form of punishment. Their questions are legitimate.

I also wanted to know—on a personal level—what is done when we apply the death penalty. I have no vested interest in proving or disproving the use of capital punishment. Mine is a personal itch. I heard a noted criminologist state, "Curiosity is a personal itch and I'll scratch it any way I damn well please." This has been my mantra. I am curious about executions. My approach is qualitative, not quantitative. I do not count them, I experience them. My methodology comes from the ethnographic tradition and uses Max Weber's expression of *verstehen*— the German word meaning "to understand."

It is not for me to judge, pontificate, or use my position to lobby for change. I am an adherent to Robert Merton's concept of "unanticipated consequences." This concept suggests that, although social scientists (and natural scientists as well) have developed enough knowledge to influence, even mandate, social change, we do not necessarily have the knowledge necessary to anticipate the consequences. This lack of predictive ability should temper our involvement in legislated social engineering and societal change.

There are those who might question, even challenge, my ethics in this research. In the long run, neither organizations nor systems should write, maintain, or enforce codes of ethics. Mine is to personally do no harm, to protect all confidences, and to fairly and honestly report what I observe. More than this I cannot do. Those on death row have confided in me and trusted me with their stories and experience, even inviting me to be present at their deaths. Those who must take these lives, in the name of the state, have confided in me and trusted me with their experiences and procedures, even letting me observe the behind-the-scenes process of execution and sharing with me their personal and professional dealings.

Field research is not easy. Were it mere observation it could perhaps be easier. However, a part of me finds its way into my notes and a part of me experiences as well as records each execution. When I am asked, "Why do you watch people die?" I answer, "So that those who don't, or can't, will understand *(verstehe)* what the process of execution entails."

ACKNOWLEDGMENTS

Because all of us are so totally indebted to so many others—in terms of who we are, what we become, and what we do—acknowledging specific individuals only creates chasms rather than building bridges. There are, however, groups and agencies I would like to thank:

- Directors, staff, and employees of the Utah State Department of Corrections
- University personnel in libraries, departments, colleges, and administration—especially at Weber State University
- Government agencies—federal, regional, and local—especially the Federal Bureau of Prisons and Senator Orrin Hatch and his administrative staff
- The men on death row and those who used to be there
- My students
- And five people I must mention by name: Barbara Lopez, my research assistant whose ability to find and retrieve everything at a moment's notice has filled in the gaps of memory and ignorance; Julie Jenkins and Carol Jensen, whose magic on the computer and unfeigned patience made completion possible; Jack Levin, who graciously introduced me to Jennifer Jacobson; and Jennifer whose company over lunch helped jump-start the process and whose encouragement helped bring it across the finish line.

I would also like to thank the following reviewers for their insight and assistance: Susan Brinkley, University of Tampa; Lisa Callahan, Russell Sage College; Stephen Owen, Radford University; Michael Perna, Nassau Community College; Jeanette Sereno, California State University, Stanislaus; Gennaro F. Vito, University of

INSIDE THE DEATH CHAMBER

CHAPTER 1

PERSONAL QUESTIONS

DO YOU HAVE NIGHTMARES FROM WATCHING PEOPLE DIE?

There were three of us standing in a small room of about fifteen square feet and the woman next to me was sobbing. We were the three witnesses chosen by the man who now lies on the gurney not ten feet in front of us. He was stretched out as though being crucified—legs together, arms outstretched. The window in front of us allowed a close view of the procedure. Through the partition next to us, the media witnesses were whispering to each other. "Is he still breathing?" "Can you see any movement?" "What is the exact time of death?"

Tom Meyer, © *San Francisco Chronicle*. Reprinted by permission.

I was prepared for the execution. I had thought through what to wear (not too formal, not too casual). What to eat before the execution. (Would I get sick if I ate too much or if I ate certain foods?) The planning process had been formal and professional. There were neither jokes nor were there any indications of punishment or vengeance. As a matter of fact, the warden had made it clear to those involved in the execution that they were to act professionally. They were carrying out their duty and they were to be as accommodating as possible to all involved—inmate, victim's family, and all others. They were not there to punish anyone, only to do their duty.

What I was not prepared for was the person next to me who was sobbing. Someone was grieving over the man being executed. It was raw emotion, something that had been left out of the planning process. Aside from the sterile setting of the actual execution, those involved—warden, staff, and inmate—had kept things on a level devoid of personal emotion and feeling. Those conducting the execution were expected to be "professional" and the one being executed was expected to "die game"—to go like a man. Everyone was "prepped" except the woman next to me.

I remember my hands getting sweaty. I was trying to remain objective and detached. I was taking notes and "documenting" what I was observing. There was not much to observe. It was a lethal injection execution. The lethal drugs had been injected, I saw his stomach rise and fall, then nothing—no twitching, struggling, no deep sighs or tremors. He was there and then he was gone.

I have witnessed six executions. Two of these were of men who, in the process of robbing a music store, killed three people, raped one, kicked a ballpoint pen into the ear of another, and made others drink Drano. Another of those executed was a serial killer who sexually molested and killed five young boys. Yet another of these executions was that of a man recently released from prison who raped and killed an 11-year-old girl on the night before her twelfth birthday. One execution I witnessed was that of a man, also just released from prison, who killed a good Samaritan who picked him up as a hitchhiker. After what he perceived to be a homosexual advance, this ex-con killed the man. Later, in one of our conversations, he explained to me that he hadn't been out of prison long enough to know he could just walk away from such a situation:

> I'm here because somebody put their hands on me. And he did it again so I killed him. I hadn't been out of prison very long and reacted the way I learned to react in prison. You had to stand up for your manhood—and quick—and firm. I didn't realize that, on the outside, I could just walk away.[1]

The sixth was Timothy McVeigh, the first federal execution after a thirty-eight-year hiatus. Four of these men chose to die. They withdrew their appeals and told the state to end their misery. Two of them battled to the end of their appeals. Five of these executions were by lethal injection, one by firing squad. I interviewed them on death row, stayed with them on the death watch, and I was present as they died.

Criminologists/Sociologists Who Witness Executions

There are others who have witnessed executions. Richard Moran, a sociologist, who witnessed the lethal injection execution of Thomas Barefoot in Texas reported:

> I had led myself to believe that death by lethal injection was a non-event. The condemned man would drift off to sleep like a hospital patient who had received general anesthesia.[2]

Instead, Moran experienced something quite different:

> I had expected to observe the execution, but I did not expect to be observed. The condemned man looked right at me. Only a few feet separated us. I was afraid he would try to touch me. . . . I was ashamed—ashamed for being there and afraid that he would ask something of me. I was an intruder, the only member of the public who had trespassed on his private moment of anguish. In my face he could see the horror of his own death.[3]

James Fox, a criminologist who witnessed the Missouri execution of Richard Zeitvogel in 1996, recorded his impressions:

> The execution itself was far less than I had expected, quite underwhelming. The State of Missouri had completely removed all the horror from the process—no smoking flesh from Ol' Sparky and no frantic struggle for air in the gas chamber.
> Lethal injection is designed to take the barbarism out of the death penalty. In my mind, it had the opposite effect. It was so straight-forward and sterile that it was just too easy. It should not be that easy to take human life.[4]

Motives for Witnessing Executions

During one of those father–son moments, my 8-year-old son asked me, "Why do you want to go watch someone die?" It was difficult then and it is difficult now to put into words. There are many people who would like to witness an execution. Some of them are curious, some looking for closure, some for sensationalism. In Florida, the more high profile the case, the more requests they get to witness the execution. Motives vary from:

- Family members who want to bring closure and complete the grief cycle. One designated family witness commented, "I'm not looking forward to watching him die. I want to see it as well as not see it. But the best step toward healing is if he gets executed.[5] After witnessing the execution of her son's killer, one mother commented, "It was easy. I'm glad it's done and glad it's over and glad he's off this earth."[6]

- Police officers who want to close the case they have been involved in. After witnessing an execution, one officer responded, "I just felt relieved. I waited for it three months short of ten years. I saw him kill a police officer, a friend of mine, not two feet in front of me."[7]

- Curiosity motivates some. A Vietnam veteran who witnessed a Florida execution said, "You get up and walk away and he's just a lump of flesh without a spirit. Some of the [other witnesses] were overwhelmed. But I was somewhat prepared."[8]

- Some criminal justice professionals want to know the consequences of their decisions. A member of the Parole and Probation Commission indicated: "I wanted to see what I was recommending. I thought I might have a better perspective. It was surrealistic. I was haunted for several days afterward. . . . The image froze of his breathing."[9] A public defender, after an execution, commented: "The ritual was the worst thing. I could just see somebody standing there saying the gods are appeased."[10]

Robert Elliott, who served as official executioner in the State of New York, as well as several other states (see Chapter 3), questioned why anyone would want to witness an execution. He stated:

> Frankly, it has always been a mystery to me why people voluntarily attend executions. Yet I know that many clamor for admittance to the death chamber every time somebody pays the extreme penalty. Sing Sing alone has a waiting list of more than a thousand would-be spectators.[11]

Reasons for Having Witnesses

In the larger context, however, there are specific reasons for having witnesses and for institutionalizing the witness role. The end of public executions prompted the need for identifiable witnesses to testify that the execution had in fact occurred. During the time when executions were held in public squares or other public areas, the public could see the process and the aftermath. They saw the condemned walk to the gallows, heard the last words, and saw the body as it was removed. When the process was moved behind prison walls, it became necessary to have witnesses who could testify that the person had in fact been executed and that the process was carried out in an appropriate manner. (See more on this in Chapter 3.)

When California added lethal injection as an option, the gurney was placed inside the famous gas chamber in San Quentin. Whereas with gas executions the condemned, in full view of the witnesses, was brought into the chamber and strapped down, the lethal injection process provided for the windows of the chamber to be covered with curtains. Behind these curtains the condemned was strapped to the gurney, the IV was inserted, and when all was ready, the curtains were opened for the witnesses to observe the rest of the procedure. Reporters took issue with the new rules and procedure. One observed, "How do we know he didn't struggle? We have to take their word for it." He continued:

> The purpose of having media witnesses is to tell the people of California exactly how an inmate is put to death. We were not allowed to see the needles inserted into the arms, we were not allowed to see the inmate escorted into the chamber. We have no idea . . . whether he struggled or went willingly. We have no way of knowing what happened.[12]

Another reporter indicated, "If the state was looking for a clean, antiseptic way to kill somebody, they found it. . . . When that curtain opened, he looked already dead."[13]

Those Who Are Required to Be Present as Witnesses

It was executioner Elliott who succinctly stated the reasons for having designated witnesses:

> Witnesses other than prison officials are usually necessary under the law. Their presence is required so they can verify that the mandate of the court was properly carried out. After the execution, they must sign a document certifying that they saw put to death the person whose name appears thereon.[14]

Consequently, there are specific directives that are generally legislatively mandated as to who can, and sometimes must, be present at an execution.

Officials.   Although regulations vary from state to state, as a rule, there are government or official witnesses whose duties require (or at least allow for) their presence. These can include the governor, state attorney's general, state and local law enforcement officials, and corrections/prison personnel.

One official, a woman magistrate whose presence was required by law, commented:

> It was a very dignified and impressive act. . . . Some might think it callous of me, but I was merely carrying out my duties as a magistrate in sinking all sentiment and human feeling. It was only a woman's duty. I was trying to prove that it was possible for a woman to take her place alongside a man in the fulfillment of public duties. In any case there was nothing to upset the susceptibilities of a woman in what I saw. I was not the least bit nervous or upset and there was not occasion for that. There was really nothing to upset a woman possessed of ordinary nerves. The enacting of one of our social laws was accomplished in solemn and decorous fashion and I cannot say that I felt any unbalancing strain in being forced to witness it.[15]

Media.   As already mentioned, another group of witnesses is the media. By statute a certain number of news media—newspapers, television, radio—are allowed to witness each execution. They must express an interest by sending a request to the department of corrections. Depending on the state, generally a pool of reporters is selected at random. Also, there is usually a pool photographer allowed.

One reporter who had witnessed several Texas lethal injection executions wrote:

> It's a very sterile environment; very quick. That's the reason I could watch so many. . . . I had to take lots of notes as fast as I could. You just set your emotions on the shelf and do your job.[16]

Another reporter who had witnessed lethal injection executions reported:

> It looks like a crucifixion; the only difference is he's lying on his back, arms spread out. . . . You're so intent on doing your job and watching for the reaction of the inmate.[17]

One reporter's reaction was similar:

> I know I'm sounding cold and emotionless, but, in there you're busy working as a reporter. You really don't have time to think about it.[18]

While preparing to witness her first electric chair execution, one reporter was given this advice: "I'll tell you what's going to bother you the most—it's that it won't bother you." She found out otherwise, "I found that to be untrue." She reported it gave her nightmares and that she was not the only one who had that reaction.[19]

Inmate's Witnesses.   A third group is the condemned's witnesses, generally three to five people of his choice—friends, family, clergy—but no other inmates. This list is carefully screened by the prison.

Timothy McVeigh asked his attorney, Robert Nigh, to be present at his execution. After the execution, Nigh commented, "We made killing a part of the healing process."[20] Other inmate-selected witnesses have included reporters, family members, and, sometimes, prison personnel.

Victim's Families.   A fourth group, again depending on the state, is a rather recent inclusion, consisting of members of the victim's family. Paul Howell, whose daughter was killed in the Oklahoma City bombing, witnessed the execution of Timothy McVeigh by closed-circuit television. He stated:

What I was hoping for, and I'm sure most of us were, we could see some kind of, maybe, "I'm sorry." You know, something like that. We didn't get anything from his face. [It] was just a big relief. . . . Just a big sigh came over my body and it felt real good.[21]

Provision is also made for a member of the clergy—either of the inmate's choosing or the prison chaplain or spiritual advisor. More will be said about this role later. It is a significant role and those who fill it are not unaffected. A member of the clergy who witnessed an electric chair execution and who actually walked the last mile with the condemned man reacted:

I pray to God I will never have to witness another execution. . . . To me these were moments detached from reality, with realism so horrifying the mind could not assimilate it. The look in the man's eyes as they placed the steel cap on his head is indelibly imprinted on my brain.[22]

Role of "Neutral Observer"

My role as witness and "neutral observer" has also become institutionalized in many states. Originally I was to be designated as a neutral observer. Such an individual has no affiliation or official connection to the process but is someone who, should questions arise or there be a need for an outsider to verify the process, can speak independently and without bias.

It used to be fairly common practice to physically "work over" the condemned the previous night so he would offer little resistance at the time of execution. Periodically there are still such accusations claiming the condemned had been injured or killed to keep him from exposing corruption or making accusatory last statements. After the 1979 execution of John Spenkelink in Florida, it was charged by his mother that he was dead when he entered the death chamber. "John was kept from making his last statement. He had too much to tell on the state," according to his mother.[23] According to news reports:

Mrs. Spenkelink said her 30-year-old son was injured and couldn't talk when he went to the preparation room before his electrocution. She claimed he had to be physically placed in the chair because he already was dead.[24]

It became necessary to exhume Spenkelink's body in order to resolve such a challenge. It is to avoid such situations that the role of "neutral observer" has been utilized.

Since my role as neutral observer had not been officially written into legislation, I was included as a witness, mostly in the role of historian but also as an official government witness. On another occasion I was there at the request of the inmate as one of his personal witnesses.

So, do I (or others) have nightmares from watching executions? What is the personal impact of being involved to this extent in the execution process? The easy answer to the question would be to deny any personal feelings. Yet, how else to explain the fact that only recently—after all these years—have I begun to go back and review my notes from each execution? Witnessing an execution has a profound effect on the observer—whether recognized at the moment or some time later. The last time I taught my death penalty class I invited a TV reporter who had been present to witness one of the same executions I had witnessed. Just a few minutes into his comments to my class he broke down. Tears rolled down his cheeks and he said, "Ten years since the execution and this is the first time I have talked about it. I did not expect this to happen."

I am fortunate. I get to talk about it often, and each time I remember the feeling. This "thing" that is done in our name is not done without cost—of life, of emotion, of many costs other than money.

QUESTIONS FOR DISCUSSION

1. Would you ever want to witness an execution? Why or why not? What if you knew the victim?
2. Do you think it is ethical to watch someone die—as a witness to his or her death?
   • as a personal witness for the condemned?
   • as a government witness?
   • as a media witness?
3. What kind of reaction do you think you would experience as a witness to an execution?
4. To what extent would you go to stop or interfere with an execution if you were opposed to capital punishment?
5. Who should be allowed to witness an execution?

THINGS TO DO OR SEE

1. Watch the movie *Dead Man Walking*. Discuss the dilemma of the nun who served as a spiritual advisor.
2. Interview someone from the media (or have him or her come to class) who has witnessed an execution.
3. Read some of the eyewitness accounts of executions as referenced in the endnotes.

ARE YOU FOR OR AGAINST
THE DEATH PENALTY?

"Are you for or against the death penalty?" I have been asked this question many times, but this time it was being asked by a death row inmate who sat across the table from me. Without waiting for my answer he continued, "I'm for it—just not in my specific case. Not for this. I've done a lot of shit I'm not proud of and things I could be in here forever for—but I'm not guilty of this."

How and where do I begin in attempting to share my personal position on the death penalty? I guess the best and only way is to be straightforward—I stand in the middle! I have no moral or religious code that requires me to oppose it. As a *sociologist*, I believe a society, particularly a democratic society, has the right to impose whatever sanctions it wishes so as to maintain the social order. On the other hand, as a *criminologist*, I find the justice system too capricious and subject to manipulation and bias to be trusted with dispensing death in a fair and equitable manner.

Perhaps my personal position is in actuality a nonposition. I have struggled and continue to struggle with many issues that impact my thinking. I have tried to immerse myself in as many aspects of the death penalty debate and the execution process as possible. I think it would be fair to say I have explored as many, or

Commutation hearing before the Utah State Board of Pardons. The author is in the background, seated, middle of the picture.
Tom Smart, © *Desert News*, Salt Lake City, UT. Reprinted by permission.

more, facets of the execution process from an academic and personal perspective as is possible. I am unimpressed with those who, on either side, make it such a simple matter—pro or con. How can anyone be either in favor of capital punishment or opposed to it? For me it cannot be that simple. And, because it is not that simple, I have had to try to balance several issues in my own mind.

Accountability

My first issue is accountability. How accountable are people for their own behavior? People I talk to tell me we are all accountable for our own actions and the choices we make. Certainly, the death penalty assumes such accountability. Yet, at the risk of being called a "misty-eyed bleeding heart," I have read the case histories and documented the childhoods of some of our most notorious criminals and I think the outcome could have been predicted.

Take the case of Robert Alton Harris, executed in California's gas chamber in 1992. Born two months prematurely because Robert's jealous father beat and kicked his pregnant wife, Robert's life continued in a world of violence. When he was a little over a year old, his father attempted to strangle him in front of his mother. While in his teens, his mother left with the rest of the family and abandoned Robert on the side of the highway. At the time of his trial medical experts testified his violent life could be attributed to fetal alcohol syndrome from his alcoholic mother.

Like Robert Harris, David Edwin Mason had a troubled past. He died in that same gas chamber in 1993. Often beaten and abused, on one occasion he was gagged and tied to a workbench after accidentally urinating on his mother. By the age of 5, after several suicide attempts including swallowing pills, choking, and setting himself on fire, he began self-mutilation by cutting and slashing himself. At the age of 8, after being repeatedly told by his mother she wished he had never been born, his room was converted to a cell—windows covered and nailed shut—where he was locked in for hours. His mother continued to beat him, one time holding a knife under his stomach and forcing him to do push-ups. By the age of 11 he had been sexually abused by several people including a teacher, another boy, and several neighborhood women who also gave him money.[25]

Although the crimes of both of these men were horrible and inexcusable, my question is who should be executed—the perpetrator, those who created the "monster," or both? Could we not have predicted a violent end in each of these situations, and was there no intervention possible?

Cause

Another issue I constantly confront is that of cause. There is a confusion in people's minds between attempts to "understand" the cause of behavior and "making excuses" for it. Let's be clear, I make no excuses! But I do want to know why. Accountability and responsibility are essential to our concepts of justice and punishment. How can we search for cause when it is considered excuse making? How can we try to find out why people kill when such attempts are perceived as efforts to justify? How then are we to proceed?

Personal Obligation

A further issue for me is a personal one. Aside from what the law says and how the government responds is the issue of my personal obligation. I have interviewed families and loved ones of many victims. I have read their accounts and, to some extent, shared their grief. This I know: Those who wait for revenge, who attend all the trials and hearings, and even many of those who attend the executions do not, as a rule, find the relief and closure they seek. In my experience and from my observations, those who forgive or at least move on with their lives, leaving the outcome to the justice system or even some higher authority—these people adjust the best.

Knowing this, I wrestle with how I should respond. In his book *The Crime of Punishment,* Karl Menninger quotes the following letter from a father whose young daughter was killed by a young neighbor:

Dear People of Philadelphia:

I write to you this morning, at the rise of dawn, still in the midst of a tormented wake, the most terrible grief which has ever seared my soul.

Yesterday afternoon, on June 4, I lost the most precious thing that life ever gave to me—a three-and-a-half-year-old girl child of surpassing purity and joy; a being profoundly close to the secret wellsprings of life itself—a closeness from which she derived great unconscious strength which made her irresistibly attractive to human beings with whom she came in contact.

She was murdered at three in the afternoon, in the basement of a house only a few doors away from ours, by a fifteen-year-old boy. . . .

The boy himself has also always given an excellent formal account of himself—honor student, gentle in manner, handsome and all the rest. . . .

I am sure that his parents have been God-fearing, upright citizens, too uneducated in matters of the human soul to have recognized the plight of their child during the years of his growth.

They undoubtedly took naive pride in his constant good behavior, neat appearance, and good performance at church and school, never suspecting that this very goodness was a serious cause of worry in the light of what must have been left unaccounted for.

It is, of course, worrisome, from the social point of view, that there are parents with such lack of understanding. It is, I submit, much more profoundly worrisome that it should have been possible for this boy to go through his whole fifteen years without anyone who was responsible for his upbringing—such as his school and his church—having taken note (out of uncaring or lack of understanding) of the danger signals before the tragedy.

Beware, citizens. The human animal cannot be cheated forever. It will have love, or kill. You will understand that I am not lecturing to you for the pure joy of sounding wise. I am hurt to the depths of my being, and I cry out to you to take better care of your children. My final word has to do with the operation of the machinery of justice. Had I caught the boy in the act, I would have wished to kill him. Now that there is no undoing of what is done, I only wish to help him.

Let no feelings of cave-man vengeance influence us. Let us rather help him who did so human a thing.

[Signed] A Sick Father[26]

To what extent are we, as human beings and members of society, entitled to revenge? How do the concepts of vengeance and retribution fit into a society based on the principle of justice?

Capriciousness of the System

On July 24, 1984, Dan and Ron Lafferty walked into the home of their sister-in-law and her baby daughter. Both of them participated in cutting the throats of the victims. Later, when tried separately, Dan developed a winking relationship with one of the female jurors who then held out during the jury's death penalty deliberations. Dan Lafferty, today, is serving a life sentence while his brother, Ron, who had no such winking relationship with the jury, sits on death row.

In January 1985, Doyle Edward Skillern died by lethal injection in Texas. He was sentenced to die because of his part in a drug deal gone bad, resulting in the death of an undercover narcotics agent. Actually, Skillern sat in the car while his partner, Charles Sanne, did the killing. Sanne admitted doing the shooting and was eligible for parole six months after Skillern's execution.[27] Skillern was sentenced to die because, under Texas law, an accomplice is considered to be equally as culpable as the actual killer—yet the actual killer was given a life sentence.

It is the capriciousness within the justice system that causes me concern. What confidence can I have that this ultimate punishment, carried out in my name, is being done fairly and equitably? How am I to reconcile the facts that:

- More men than women are executed.
- More poor and lower class than affluent end up on death row.
- More killers with white victims than those with other racial/ethnic victims are sentenced to die.

During one of my interviews on death row, the condemned inmate, talking about the inherent bias within the system, said to me, "Look around you. We are not the cold-blooded, premeditated murderers we are made out to be. We are here because we are stupid. If my partner and I had planned out our crime we wouldn't be here. Instead, things just escalated and we ended up killing those people."

As I thought about it, this statement seemed to have some merit. Among the "blood-thirsty" and "cold-blooded" murderers, the most successful who repeat their crimes most frequently are seldom, if ever, caught and brought to justice—professional hit men for organized crime, professional assassins hired by governments or governmental agencies. Somehow, through the media, politicians, or otherwise, the public has been sold the image of the murderer as the bogey man—lurking, leering, and constantly repeating the crime. The reality is:

- Most murderers do not repeat their crimes.
- Murderers are the best risk on parole.
- Murderers are, as a rule, the best behaved in prison.
- Most murders are acts of passion, not carefully premeditated crimes.

And, therefore, I question myself as to why we are executing these people. I have known many murderers—some of them I distrust totally, others I have come to respect. Are all expendable? Unredeemable?

There are many people who believe the only legitimate position for an educated and enlightened person is an anti–death penalty stance. I certainly don't hold that position. In the end, capital punishment is an emotional issue and whatever position a person takes is essentially an emotional position—not a scientific one. Science has not been able to answer the questions of deterrence, morality, right or wrong, and so on. As a matter of fact, one researcher stated:

> Ultimately, virtually all countries that have abolished the death penalty have done so because of changing attitudes about the morality and ethics of capital punishment—not academic debates. There is nowhere in the world where abolition has occurred because of the scientific findings.[28]

I stand in the middle. My knowledge, observations, and experience have only made me more tentative about taking an absolute position for or against.

QUESTIONS FOR DISCUSSION

1. What is your personal position on the death penalty?
2. On what factors do you base your opinion?
3. Specifically address the other questions raised throughout this chapter.

THINGS TO DO OR SEE

1. Get in small groups and discuss everyone's opinions on the death penalty.
2. Have various members of the class stand and present their opinions and experiences.
3. Hold a class debate on capital punishment—pro versus con.

CHAPTER 2

GENERAL QUESTIONS

WHY ARE THERE 13 STEPS TO THE GALLOWS? (MAGIC, SUPERSTITION, AND RITUAL)

I recently stood over a small plaque marking the location of London's Tyburn gallows. It is on a small island in the middle of a busy intersection across from Marble Arch. It was to Tyburn the condemned were taken by cart from Newgate Prison. The handbell, which can still be seen today, from old St. Sepulchre would ring as they left the prison. As a part of the ritual, the night before each execution, and the morning of, the bellman from St. Sepulchre would chant:

> All you that in the condemned hold do lie,
> Prepare you, for tomorrow you shall die;
> Watch, all, and pray, the hour is drawing near
> That you before the Almighty must appear;
> Examine well yourselves, in time repent,
> That you may not to t'etrnal flames be sent.
> And when St. Sepulchre's Bell to-morrow tolls,
> The Lord have mercy on your souls!
> Past twelve o'clock![1]

Amid taunts and jeers, and with frequent stops at pubs along the way, the condemned eventually arrived at Tyburn—the triple tree, the deadly never-green, the three-legged mare, the triangular gallows. Death at this place was referred to as "riding of a horse foaled by an acorn."[2] Tremendous crowds had gathered and the festivities and celebration at this famous gallows gave birth to our present-day word *gala*, describing a celebration of great proportion—reminiscent of public executions. Many common usages, symbols, and superstitions in our modern society can be traced to executions.

Superstitions about the Hangman

Hangmen occupied unique positions in medieval Europe. Shaking hands with a hangman, on the one hand, was believed to bring bad luck, whereas, on the other hand, it was supposed to have certain curative powers. Seeing a hangman could be unlucky or warn of bad news. Walking under a ladder was believed to bring bad luck. Ladders were symbols of execution and, thus, walking under one could only portend evil consequences. In France, hangmen wore coats of red with an embroidered ladder to designate their profession. Executioners, to avoid any potential evil that might befall them as a result of their work, would spit between the rungs of a ladder. This fear of consequences also applied to their belief in the next life. Consequently, the hangman always shook hands with the condemned and asked forgiveness from them prior to the execution. Hangmen were entitled to the clothing of the condemned and could sell them for profit after each execution. They also sold pieces of the rope—believed to have curative powers. One hangman sold the rope for $1 per inch and was known to have three ropes for each execution so as to increase his profits. It was also not unusual for the hangman, for a price, to allow citizens to touch the hand of a newly executed person. It was believed this touch would cure warts and other blemishes. It was also believed that, by placing the finger of an executed thief under the threshold of their home, it could be protected from theft. Hangmen were also the early medicine men in that they created and sold ointments made from the blood, hair, and other ingredients obtained in the execution process.

Hangmen, however, also saw themselves as providing a service—not only to the sovereign and the public but to the condemned. Some made sure there was a hole in the hood placed over the head of those about to be executed so that there was a place for the spirit to escape. They also believe they heard the last "honest" confession of each person who was prepared to die. Executioner James Berry stated, "They never tell lies to the hangman."[3] It was Berry's own superstition that provided he would never hang a person facing east. He and another executioner, Marwood, made sure the knot was placed behind the left ear—since the left represented the "sinister" side of the person. A more recent executioner felt relief at the condemned's confession, seeing it as an expiation of his own guilt in the process:

> What makes me feel psychologically good is when I am putting the rope around the convict's neck, I hear him muttering his last words: "Forgive me, God. Forgive me, God." These words indicate he is guilty.[4]

Enduring Superstitions

Many superstitions have developed among the public and are still prevalent today. Already mentioned is the bad luck from walking under a ladder. In addition, placing one's shoes on the table was a symbol of hanging. A stiff neck was an omen that a person is about to be hanged. Dreaming of a hanged person meant a person was about to have a pleasant surprise.

The number thirteen has been considered an unlucky number since early Christian traditions marked the number as representing those present at Christ's last supper. Friday, as an unlucky day, can also be traced back to the day Christ was crucified. Friday the 13th has been a double-whammy when it comes to bad luck. For this reason, some contend, executions were traditionally carried out on Fridays. Thirteen has been used symbolically in executions as well. On a recent visit to Folsom's old gallows room I actually counted thirteen steps from the floor to the platform where the condemned stood. Traditionally, it was believed there were thirteen steps to the gallows and, in the old "western knot" used for hangings in the "old west" there were thirteen coils in the knot. As a child growing up in the West, I was taught it was illegal to tie a hangman's noose—which made it all the more of a challenge. My friends and I became quite adept at this illegal activity. The truth is, the hangman's knot is generally tied with only eight or nine coils.

Among other superstitions were those associated with the colors black (and white) as symbols of sadness, grief, and doom. These colors were used extensively in the execution process. The sheets (or shrouds) used to wrap the condemned prior to execution were traditionally white or black, as were the hoods used to cover the heads. Hangmen often wore either white or black gloves. In a double firing squad conducted in Utah in 1956, two firing squads were used simultaneously with the condemned sitting in two chairs—one white (for sorrow) and one black (for death).

Additionally, elm trees were considered unlucky as they were used for hangings. And, on the gallows, a horseshoe, generally considered a symbol of luck, was hung upside down symbolizing the condemned's luck had run out.

Double firing squad with two chairs—one white and one black.
Used by permission, Utah State Historical Society, all rights reserved.

Words and Expressions

There are several common expressions in the English language that also trace their roots to the execution process. The origin of the word *derrick*, a contraption used to lift and stack hay, takes its name from one of England's first hangmen. Referred to only as Derrick, he is known for being the one who executed the Earl of Essex in the Tower of London in 1601. Essex had saved Derrick from execution for an earlier offense deserving of the death penalty:

> In accordance with the custom of the time, the Earl did so on condition that Derrick serve as an executioner. Scott mentions Derrick in *The Fortunes of Nigel*, and the hangman gave his name to the type of crane called a derrick because of its resemblance to the gallows he used. (The gallows itself was known sometimes as a "derrick" in the reign of James I.)[5]

It is not unusual to hear people say, "I'll be hanged if I will," or "Give him enough rope and he will hang himself." The phrase "giving people enough rope" is not only a figure of speech, but it also has its origins in the amount of slack provided in the rope prior to hanging. Other phrases are less easily attributed to their origins in the execution genre. "Sticking out one's neck" is a reference to hanging, as is being "caught napping" or he "napped it." "Toeing the mark" originally referred to the condemned being moved so that their toes were on the specific mark on the trap door before they were dropped. "Pulling your leg" referred to the days of quartering the condemned where not only was the person hanged, until almost dead, but also then drawn and quartered. Some have also suggested that this refers to the "humane" practice of hangmen allowing friends or relatives of the condemned to wait underneath the gallows in order to pull on the legs to assure the neck was broken and ensure a quicker death. "Going west" became a term for dying and originated from the westerly trip of the condemned from Newgate Prison to Tyburn.

It seems, wherever I look, there are words, symbols, and superstitions that trace their origins to executions and the application of the death penalty throughout history. I am neither crazy nor possessed but I have found a deeper sense of my own life and a greater appreciation for the life of others as I have studied the execution process. When an execution occurs anywhere in the world, but especially in my state, I know my hand is on the rope. As was done in Halifax:

> when the offender hath made his confession, and hath laid his neck over the nethermost block, every man there present doth either take hold of the rope (or putteth forth his arm so near to the same as he can get in token that he is willing to see justice executed) and pulling out the pin [pulling the trigger, inserting the needle, dropping the pellets, etc.] in this manner.[6]

QUESTIONS FOR DISCUSSION

1. Are you superstitious?
2. Would you be hesitant to shake the hand or associate with a person if you knew he or she was an executioner?
3. Do you think those involved in the execution process carry with them any stigma of evil or bad luck?
4. Do you think there is any validity to any of these superstitions?
5. Do you agree with the Halifax Gibbet Law? Should judges and members of juries be required to witness the executions of those they sentence?

THINGS TO DO OR SEE

1. Ask people about their superstitions. What ones do they have? Why do they or do they not walk under ladders? Are they aware of the source of their superstitions?
2. Can you think of other superstitions that can be traced to executions or executioners?

WHY HAVE ANIMALS AND INANIMATE OBJECTS BEEN EXECUTED?

I recently located the execution site of a horse, executed in Utah in 1854. It seems a young soldier was caught having a rather "intimate" relationship with his mare. Both were sentenced to die by firing squad. On the day of the execution, the governor met with the young man and agreed to commute his sentence if he would leave the territory and never return. The young man left and the horse was taken out and shot.[7]

On my wall is the picture of "Murderous Mary." News reports referred to her hanging as drawing the largest crowd ever assembled in Erwin, Tennessee. The picture in the newspaper shows her hanging. The date was September 13, 1916.

Mary was a circus elephant with a bad temper. While preparing for the circus parade, her trainer took her to get some water. Spotting a discarded watermelon, she headed straight for it. When the trainer tried to turn her, she grabbed him and threw him into a drink stand and then stomped on his head. They got her calmed down enough to perform that evening but in the next town she attacked the circus manager and they decided to hang her.

Murderous Mary, the five-ton elephant, was hanged from a one-hundred-ton railroad derrick. (Note the use of this term from the previous chapter.) The first attempt failed when the chain broke, but they got a stronger chain the

*"Murderous Mary" hanging from a railroad derrick in
Erwin, Tennessee.*
Courtesy of Tennessee State Library and Archives.

second time. One of the witnesses stated: "I don't believe any of those who saw the
event felt it was inhumane. Mary paid for her crimes just as anyone else would."[8]

This statement reflects the thinking of an earlier time when animals and
inanimate objects were imbued with human characteristics and, like humans,
could be possessed and influenced by evil spirits.

The Judeo-Christian admonition under the Law of Moses mandated if an
ox gored a man it should be stoned. In the Athenian culture, the Law of Drakon
and Erechtheus required any weapons used in the death of an individual be "publicly condemned and thrown beyond the Athenian borders."[9] A statue to honor
the great athlete Nikon was sentenced by Athenians to be thrown into the sea because it had toppled from its pedestal and killed someone. Plato advocated for the
execution of animals and inanimate objects:

> If a draught animal or any other beast kill a person . . . the kinsmen of the slain shall
> prosecute the said homicide for murder.[10]

There are many historical examples of the application of these policies:

Animals

In 1864 at Pleternica, Slavonia, a pig was tried and executed. It seems this pig had eaten the ears of a 1-year-old girl. Not only was the guilty pig punished, but the "head" pig was required to provide a dowry for the mutilated girl, "so that the loss of her ears might not prove to be an insuperable obstacle to her marriage."[11]

In 1314, a bull from Moisy, France, got loose onto a highway and killed a man. The bull was tried, convicted, and hanged from the public gallows.[12]

In 1474, a cock, guilty of the unnatural act of laying an egg, was burned at the stake.[13]

Inanimate Objects

In the Islands of Scotland, it is often the custom to abandon on the beach a boat from which a fisherman has drowned. The assumption is that the boat is "guilty of manslaughter and must no longer be permitted to sail the sea with innocent craft."[14]

In 1591, the great town bell of Uglich was rung to signal the beginning of a rebellion that resulted in the death of an exiled Russian prince. As a punishment the bell was exiled to Siberia and only after 300 years of banishment and "solitary confinement" was it purged and returned to its original tower in Uglich.[15]

In Fouchow, China, for causing the death of a ranking military official, fifteen wooden idols were decapitated and thrown in a pond—after being duly tried and sentenced.[16]

Trials and Confessions

In some instances animals were put on the rack or experienced other forms of torture to exact a confession. They were generally given due process, even to the extent of introducing evidence of good character. In the case of a "she-ass" discovered in an act of "buggery" with her master, he was sentenced to die, but she was acquitted. It was argued she did not participate of her own free will. Additionally, the court received a letter from the prior of the local convent stating, "they had known the said she-ass for four years, and that she had always shown herself to be virtuous and well-behaved both at home and abroad and had never given occasion of scandal to any one," and that, therefore, "they were willing to bear witness that she is in word and deed and in all her habits of life a most honest creature."[17]

During trial and when executed it was not uncommon for the accused beast to be dressed in human clothes. In 1386, a sow who had killed a young child was sentenced to be tortured and maimed, then hanged. She was dressed in human clothes and executed in the town square. Periodically there were attempts at deterrence. In one instance of a pig's trial and execution in 1457 in Lavegny, France, a sow and her six piglets were charged with murdering and partly eating a child. The sow was sentenced to die, but the piglets, because of "their youth [and] the bad example of their mother," were acquitted.[18] Sometimes the bodies of such executed animals were either displayed in public places or burned, scattered, or buried at crossroads so the evil that possessed them could not return to its original haunts.

Other instances of animal executions include the execution of goats and cows as well as the punishment of rats, bees, weevils, locusts, serpents, caterpillars, horse flies, Spanish flies, and worms—all at the hands of the state. There is even the recorded example of an entire orchard being punished by "anathema" (a curse pronounced against it) because "its fruits were tempting the children."[19]

The various forms of punishment, including capital punishment, are always based on some assumptions, explicit or implicit, about the cause of behavior and the concomitant effect of such punishment. Our early forefathers, as exhibited earlier, based their punishments on superstition and/or religious belief about the nature of humans, animals, and inanimate objects and on the culpability of each.

Benefit of Clergy

Although there was supposedly one law for all, it was possible for priests and other religious leaders to claim "benefit of clergy" and, thus, be tried under a separate, more lenient ecclesiastical law as a first offender. To qualify for the benefit of clergy it was necessary to quote what came to be known as the "neck verse," which was taken from Psalm 51 of the Old Testament:

> Have mercy upon me, O God, according to thy loving-kindness: according unto the multitude of thy tender mercies blot out my transgressions. Wash me thoroughly from mine inequity, cleanse me from my sin. For I acknowledge my transgressions: and my sin is ever before me.[20]

According to Hugo Bedau:

> Benefit of clergy arose from the struggle between church and state in England, and it originally provided that priests, monks and other clerics were to be remanded from secular to ecclesiastical jurisdiction for the trial on indictment of felony. In later centuries, this privilege was applied by ordinary criminal courts to more and more persons and for ever larger number of felonies. Eventually, all persons accused of capital crimes were spared a death sentence if the crime was a first felony offense and if it was clergyable, provided only the criminal could recite the "neck verse" this being construed by the court as proof of his literate (and thus clerical) status. Benefit of clergy became, in effect, the fictional device whereby first offenders were given a lesser punishment.[21]

Interestingly enough, this was one of the issues that had to be settled prior to the trial of an animal. Was it to be considered a lay "person"? If so, there could be no benefit of clergy. However, if a case could be made for clerical status—and I'm not sure how that would be accomplished—then benefit of clergy was a possibility for animals as well. I'm not sure, however, how they were to quote the "neck verse."

Evil Spirits and Evil Places

The punishment of animals was seen as a protection from the evil spirits to which they were believed to be susceptible. These evil spirits were believed to enter the bodies of domestic animals and household pets. Their presence was proof of the reality of sin and the influence of evil in a family or community. Such a presence had to be eliminated and destroyed.

Aside from the actual execution of animals to get rid of such evil, the culprits (animals as well as humans) were often returned to the site of the crime to meet their deaths. The belief was that evil haunted the specific location of the crime and, unless expiated, would continue to influence whomever lived there or passed by. In the earlier history of the West, the condemned were often taken by wagon to the scene of the crime and executed—sometimes even sitting on their coffins and sometimes buried where they were executed.

Condemned man sitting on his coffin prior to being executed by firing squad at the scene of his crime.
Used by permission, Utah State Historical Society, all rights reserved.

If such expiation did not occur, it was also a possibility that famine, pestilence, and destruction would visit the area.

Culpability

Although it is difficult, now, to understand the context in which anyone could consider the punishment and execution of animals, there is a convoluted logic put forth by one jurist's theory of the personification of animals:

> As only human beings can commit crime and thus render himself liable to punishment, he [the author] concludes that it is only by an act of personification that the brute can be placed in the same category of man and become subject to the same penalty.[22]

The logic, then, runs as follows—religion (or superstition or law) sets forth the requirement that animals must pay for their crimes. There may be some question as to the culpability of these animals so, to make it more palatable, animals are given human attributes and characteristics. These characteristics are symbolized by clothing and emotion, thus making animals accountable to the same degree that humans are.

The challenge for anyone looking at things historical is to understand them from the perspective of the times in which they occurred. The attempt to discover causes of behavior has evolved over a long period of time. Some would argue that our modern study of criminology in attempting to find cause is still struggling and may even reflect the bias of our modern paradigm rather than the "reality" of causation. Evans, writing in 1906, reminds us:

> It must be remembered . . . that, although the savage spirit of revenge, that eagerly demands blood for blood without the slightest consideration of the anatomical, physiological or psychological conditions upon which the commission of the specific act depends, has ceased to be the controlling factor in the enactment and execution of penal codes; the new system of jurisprudence, based upon more enlightened conceptions of human responsibility, is still in an inchoate state and very far from having worked out satisfactory solution of the intricate problem of the origin and nature of crime and its proper penalty.[23]

Personification and "Disneyfication" of Animals and Inanimate Objects

Today, in our society, we have turned again, in many ways, to the theory of the personification of animals and inanimate objects—imbuing them with human characteristics, feelings, and emotions. Disney has given us a host of animal characters with emotions including Thumper, Bambi, the Lion King, and Fivel. Pet rocks, eggs, and mechanical "babies" now *need* to be "loved," "petted," and "nourished." We have not quite reached the point of assigning culpability, but if a rock has needs and if animals have emotions, in today's society, how far are we from holding them culpable? We do put to death (execute?) dogs that attack children, grizzlies that attack campers, and livestock that carry disease. If we find that music and lyrics have influence over human emotions, how long until we extend that influence to include animals and inanimate objects? If chemicals, television, and video games influence behavior or bring an "evil" influence to the behavior of our children, how long until we "banish" them? And, if guns are held to be accountable for the deaths they cause, how long until we punish the guns, these inanimate objects, by destruction or legal "anathema"?

It has been said:

> The puzzling knots, which we seek painfully to untie and succeed only in helplessly tangling, they [our ancestors] boldly cut with the executioner's sword.[24]

Perhaps things were simpler then, and we, although attempting to resolve things in a more humane and enlightened way, have only made them more complicated.

QUESTIONS FOR DISCUSSION

1. What is culpability and how is it assigned?
2. Are animals and inanimate objects ever culpable for their actions? Under what circumstances would you assign culpability to an animal or inanimate object?
3. Why do we euthanize dogs, cats, and other animals that attack humans? Would you consider this a form of execution?
4. Have you ever kicked (or stared at) a rock or tree root you stumbled over?
5. To what extent do you believe the anthropomorphism of animals and inanimate objects could contribute to a heightened sense of culpability?

THINGS TO DO OR SEE

1. Collect and read newspaper and magazine articles in which culpability is implied—euthanized pets, wild animals, and so on.
2. Watch television, movies, and children's programs and identify the extent to which inanimate objects are given human characteristics. Discuss, as a class, the impact such characterizations might have on culpability.

HOW MANY WOMEN HAVE BEEN EXECUTED
IN THE UNITED STATES?

They are not "my ladies," although some people have referred to them as such. I feel I know them all. I have read their letters, their last words, and I know how they spent their last hours. I have interviewed some of their children—and I am still trying to contact others. Some of these women I have corresponded with while they were on death row.

Their stories are tragic and heartbreaking. Their pictures look down from my office wall as I write. Each picture has its own story to tell.[25]

"My Ladies"

New York's Eva Coo (a.k.a. Little Eva, The Witch of Crumhorn Mountain, The Roadhouse Queen) smiles at me from under her straw hat. I can't even imagine what it must have been like when the body of her victim, and hired hand, "Gimpy," was dug up, six days after his death. Eva was taken back to the scene of the crime on Crumhorn Mountain and there forced to reenact the crime with Gimpy's corpse in an attempt by the police and prosecution to coerce a confession. Eva Coo was executed in Sing Sing's "Old Sparky" on June 27, 1934.

The picture of New York's Mary Francis Creighton is also on my wall. Her eyes are wide open and there is a hint of a smile, neither of which was true at the time of her execution. She and Everett Applegate were sentenced to die for killing Applegate's 300-pound wife. Creighton, as far as I can tell, was totally unaware of her execution. After eating a bowl of ice cream for her last meal, and just thirty minutes before her scheduled execution, she passed out and never regained consciousness. According to news accounts, upon entering the death chamber, she showed no evidence of life:

> Twenty-four official witnesses agreed she was unconscious. Her head lolled limply over her right shoulder. Her eyes were closed. Her fat cheeks, once notable for their rosy color but now chalk white, sagged heavily into the creases of her neck.[26]

Unconscious and unaware, she was strapped in "Old Sparky" and died in the green room July 16, 1935.

Louisiana's Ada LeBoeuf was hanged February 1, 1929. The picture on my wall shows her as she is carried into the courtroom on a bed because her health was bad and she was subject to fainting spells. Apparently her health had been good enough to go pirogueing with her husband one night. He never returned from that boat ride. His body was later discovered in Lake Palourde by two frog hunters. He had been slit from "gullet to groin" and weighted down with angle iron. Hence, the popular song of the day, "Sweet Pirogueing Mama, don't you angle iron me." Louisiana young men, when asking for a date, would even invite their sweethearts to go pirogueing. Ada and her codefendant, "Doc" Dreher, were both sentenced to die and hanged for her husband's murder.

My picture of Arizona's Eva Dugan is unique. I took it myself in the Pinal County Museum in Florence, Arizona. It is her mug shot, taken when she entered the prison to await her execution, and it is framed with the rope that was used to hang her. Her picture is not the only one. There are seventeen in all, and all framed with the ropes with which the condemned were hanged. Her picture is the only one of a woman—the last woman hanged in Arizona. She was sentenced to die for killing the rancher for whom she worked. The real culprit was probably "Jack," the hired hand, but he ran off and was never found. Eva was charged with murder after her arrest for trying to sell the rancher's car. Eva spent her time on death row sewing her own burial clothes and passing the hat so she could pay for her own burial plot.

Probably the most touching picture on my wall is that of Barbara Graham. She is holding her 2-year-old son Tommy, shortly before her execution. It was on Tommy's head that she swore her innocence. She died in California's gas chamber at San Quentin along with two men who implicated her in the killing of an elderly woman whom they had robbed. It has been suggested they involved her because they believed California would not execute a woman and, if the state would not execute her, then the two of them would not be executed either.

Barbara Graham holding her two-year-old son Tommy prior to her execution.
AP/Wide World Photo. Reprinted by permission.

Some say her last words were, "Good people are always so sure they're right." Most likely, however, her last words were those spoken to the assistant warden who, after she was strapped into Chair A in the gas chamber, told her if she held her breath until the gas fumes were around her neck and then took a deep breath, it wouldn't hurt so much. She responded, "How the hell would you know."

There are other pictures on my wall. Those mentioned are just a few. So many stories, so many images. Thirty-nine women were executed in the United States during the twentieth century. They were women and mothers—as well as killers.

Why Women Kill

As women, their crimes were not all that different from men. Some of them killed their children or relatives and others killed in the commission of other crimes. It is generally assumed that for a woman to be deserving of the death penalty her crime must be one of a most heinous nature—involving either a large number of victims, a most bloody and cruel killing, or a totally selfish act at the expense of all those around her. Upon closer examination, however, these assumptions don't hold up.

Some of the crimes committed by these executed women either defy description, appear unbelievably stupid, or make no sense at all:

- In South Carolina, Sue Logue's husband was killed by a neighbor in an argument over a calf. The neighbor stood trial and was acquitted. Logue and her brother-in-law planned the killing of this neighbor and hired a person to do it. After the killing, the sheriff and one of his deputies arrived at the Logue home to arrest them. Both officers were killed and the trio was brought to trial and executed.
- California's Louise Peete, on parole after serving a sentence for another murder, deceived the couple she was living with—killing the woman and having her husband committed to a mental hospital—then mailed glowing reports of her progress on parole. These reports caused suspicion and she was eventually arrested, tried, and executed in California's gas chamber.
- Also in California, Elizabeth Duncan, out of jealousy, hired two men to kill her pregnant daughter-in-law. Because she had attempted to hire several other people to do the killing, she was easily traced, eventually arrested, tried, and executed.
- New York's Ruth Snyder (a.k.a. The Iron Widow, Granite Woman) convinced her lover to personally test a variety of drugs and poisons before deciding on physical violence as the preferred method of disposing of her husband. She and her accomplice brought six different weapons (rope, necktie, poisons, sash weight, piano wire, and towel) with them in order to accomplish her husband's death. Both died in Sing Sing's "Old Sparky."

It is also generally assumed these women kill because the men in their lives use them and involve them as accomplices in male-manipulated crimes. The precipitating factors leading to their crimes have not always been clear. It is not always easy to identify the actual motives. The press, the public, and prosecuting attorneys all have a hand in presenting various ideas of what the motives were. Over all, there seems to be a preponderance of killings for insurance money—particularly during the 1930s, 1940s, and 1950s.

■ New York's Anna Antonio had her brother killed on the day before his wedding so she would still be the beneficiary of his insurance policy.
■ Delaware's May Cary had her two sons assist her in the killing of her brother for his insurance. She promised the older son (who was executed with her) a car if he would help her.
■ New York's Eva Coo was charged with hitting her handyman on the head with a mallet and driving over him with an automobile, with her female accomplice, to obtain his insurance policy of $3,000.

There were, of course, several other possible motives:

Love—Louisiana's Toni Jo Henry was executed for killing a traveling salesman on her way to break her husband, "Cowboy" Henry, out of prison.

Rage—Alabama's Selina Gilmore became angry when her order of fried brains was not served promptly. She was kicked out of the café and returned later with a shotgun, killing the waiter.

Ideology—Ethel Rosenberg was electrocuted, along with her husband, for selling atomic secrets to the Russians.

Drugs—North Carolina's Velma Barfield became the first woman executed by lethal injection for the poisonings of her mother, fiancé, and two employers in order to conceal her theft of money to support her prescription drug habit.

What impact these motives had on whether these women received the death penalty is not clear. There were obviously some economic elements involved in that the insurance industry was relatively new. Many people were unemployed or struggling, and resentment certainly could have been high regarding women who killed for money.

As to the role of accomplices, in the cases of these women, it was frequently the accomplices who testified against them. Of the crimes committed by these women, there were a total of forty-six accomplices. Eleven of these women had no accomplice but acted alone in their crimes. When there were accomplices, these included hired hit men, acquaintances, friends, lovers, brothers, brothers-in-law, and their own children. All but three of the accomplices were men:

- California's Juanita Spinelli's daughter "Gypsy" was charged, along with her mother, in the killing of Robert Sherrod, a member of their gang of criminals.
- New York's Eva Coo had her friend Martha Clift drive the automobile that killed her handyman.
- North Carolina's Bessie Mae Williams was present but took no part in killing a cab driver. The female accomplice who actually did participate was a juvenile and was not executed because of her age.

The eleven women who used no accomplices were mostly poisoners, although there were other crimes as well:

- Florida's Betty Butler killed a woman who proposed a lesbian affair while they were boating on a lake.
- Alabama's Rhonda Belle Martin poisoned two husbands, three of her children, and her mother.
- New York's Mary Farmer killed her rich neighbor to obtain enough property to make her new baby rich when he grew up.
- Florida's Judi Buenoano was charged with attempting to kill her fiancé in a car bombing, drowning her paralyzed 19-year-old son by pushing him out of a canoe, and possibly poisoning one husband and one live-in boyfriend.
- Georgia's Lena Baker killed the grist mill operator she was living with because of the alleged abuses she received.

Of the forty-six accomplices involved, twenty-five of them were executed. In some instances the accomplices had arranged plea bargains and made deals with the prosecution. In others, the accomplices were never found or were expected to exonerate the women at the last moment.

Eva Dugan waited expectantly for her accomplice, know only as "Jack," to ride in on a white horse and save her. He never showed up, but just prior to her execution, she received a postcard, which simply read, "Well, that was some little failure, wasn't it?" It was signed, "Lovingly, Jack."

Several of these women were offered deals to implicate their accomplices. Barbara Graham, Bonny Brown Heady, and Dovie Dean all were offered special arrangements (presumably life in prison instead of execution) if they would sign confessions or other papers dealing with their crimes. Each refused.

Last Words, Last Meals, and What They Wore

Although on the one hand the press treated these women as anomalies of their sex, on the other hand they were portrayed in stereotypical gender roles. Their last meals were noted; their last words recorded; their dress commented on and sometimes critiqued.

Nathan Rice, warden at North Carolina's Central Prison, told me Velma Barfield, executed in 1984, had a Coke and a KitKat candy bar for her last meal. Others have chosen extensive meals, such as Dovie Dean, executed in 1954 for killing her husband with rat poison. For her last meal she ate roast chicken, potatoes, asparagus, a green salad with French dressing, coconut cream pie, angel food cake, and coffee. Some have had simple fare. Elizabeth Duncan, executed in California in 1958, chose steak and salad. Karla Faye Tucker, executed in Texas in 1998 for an axe killing, ate sliced peaches, a banana, and a green salad. Ruth Snyder, executed in New York in 1929 for killing her husband, was not even asked what she wanted for her last meal. The warden felt asking her would make her hysterical because it would remind her it was going to be her last meal. Eva Dugan, executed in Arizona in 1930, prepared her own last meal of oyster stew on a small hot plate in her cell.

As a rule, the last words of these women have been for their families, for forgiveness, or words of admonition and caution to others who might follow in their footsteps. Irene Schroeder (Iron Irene), executed in Pennsylvania in 1931 for killing a highway patrolman, directed her last words at those who prepared meals for her codefendant Glenn Dague. "Tell them in the kitchen to fry Glenn's eggs on both sides. He likes them that way."

Many, as they spoke their last words, were focused on the next life. Bessie Mae Williams said, "God has answered my prayers. I'm ready now." From the gallows May Carey said, "My way is clear; I have nothing else to say." Mary Farmer intoned, "Jesus, Mary, and Joseph, have mercy on my soul." Ruth Snyder quoted, "Father forgive them for they know not what they do."

Others, like Martha Jule Beck, lamented, "I know my sin was great, but the penalty is great too. That makes things even I guess." Rhonda Belle Martin left a note bequeathing her body to science in order to "see if someone can find out why I committed the crimes I have committed. I can't understand it, for I had no reason whatsoever." And Anna Marie Hahn, in her last words, was looking for a way out as she looked around the execution chamber and pleaded, "Isn't there anybody who will help me? Is nobody going to help me?"

Modesty

Bonnie Brown Heady was executed in Missouri's gas chamber seated next to her codefendant, Carl Hall, for kidnaping and killing 6-year-old Bobby Greenlease. As they were both being strapped in the chair, her last words were for his comfort. She asked, "You got plenty of room, honey?" and he replied, "Yes, Mamma."[27] Then, to underscore her femininity and her modesty, she asked, "Is my dress pulled down?"[28]

As a rule, prisons did everything in their power to protect the modesty of women being executed. It was England's Mary Blandy who, upon mounting the gallows, admonished, "Gentlemen, don't hang me high for the sake of decency."[29]

In the United States, when a woman was executed, she was generally attended by prison matrons who had been with her throughout her stay on death row. They accompanied her to the execution chamber and usually positioned themselves directly between her and the mostly male witnesses and press—for "the sake of decency."

In the case of the execution of Ruth Snyder, this shield of decency failed. As Snyder was being strapped in, one of the matrons assigned to stand in front of her fainted and had to be helped out of the execution chamber. This left Ruth unprotected and exposed. The following day, a reporter describing Ruth Snyder's execution commented that she wore "blue bloomers." It was also because of this fainting matron that the famous picture of Ruth Snyder (see page 77), taken the moment the switch was thrown, appeared on the front page of the *New York Daily News*. (See more on this story in Chapter 3.)

The public and the press have closely followed what women wear to their executions. In his book *Lord High Executioner*, Engel reports that Ann Turner, executed in England in 1615, had created the fashion of yellow starch in cuffs, collars, and ruffles. Later, as a result of political intrigues, she was hanged wearing yellow-dyed cuffs and ruffs. The hangmen wore the same. This apparently brought an end to this particular fashion. Marie Manning, in 1849 wore black satin to the gallows and became known as "the woman who murdered black satin." After her execution, there was little to no market for black satin.

In the United States there has been a variety of execution fashions for women. In many instances prison regulations mandated prison garb. In some instances the women were allowed to select, even create, their own ensemble. There have obviously been certain guidelines and restrictions. For example, the wearing of dresses was discontinued when it was discovered that it took longer for women to die in the gas chamber than for men. A little research pointed to the fact that the gas got trapped under the women's dresses, thus taking it longer to reach their nostrils.

In 1984, Velma Barfield wore pink pajamas and blue house slippers to her lethal injection execution in North Carolina. Judi Buenoano wore dark blue slacks and a white shirt to her 1998 execution in Florida. Barbara Graham died in San Quentin's gas chamber wearing a beige wool suit, brown pumps, and shiny baubles for earrings. In that same gas chamber, Louise Peete (The Dowager of Tahachapi) wore a gray and burgundy print dress, and Elizabeth Duncan wore a red and white striped seersucker prison dress. Ruth Snyder had asked permission to wear a black silk dress but instead wore a khaki-colored smock. Other forms of dress, as reported in various accounts of their executions, include:

Imitation silk dress, gray in color with white collar and cuffs, beige silk stockings, and black satin slippers. (Irene Schroeder, February 23, 1931)

Blue cotton pajamas and a brown silk robe. (Anna Marie Hahn, December 7, 1938)

Pink and black print dress, white oxfords, and bobby socks. (Betty Butler, June 12, 1954)

Green button-down-the-front dress, brown shoes with white anklets. (Dovie Dean, January 15, 1954)

A black dress with a touch of white at the collar, black stockings, and black shoes. (May Carey, June 7, 1935)

Regardless of how they died or even what crimes they committed, most of these women were mothers and their last thoughts were for their children. Sometimes, as in the case of one Nevada woman awaiting execution, her children were allowed to stay with her up to the time of execution. Pregnant women were allowed to deliver their children while awaiting death, and new mothers kept their young children with them. Others, whose children were older, spent their last hours thinking of their children:

Irene Schroeder spent her last days writing her life history to be sold after her death to raise money for her 6-year-old son, Donnie. She also left a letter to be given to him when he was old enough to understand (as did Ruth Snyder, Mary Farmer, and several others).

Ada LeBoeuf had been unable to have a last visit with her crippled mother. As "Miss Ada" was led to the gallows, her final words were, "My mother! My mother! Oh, my God, isn't this a terrible thing?" After her execution, her 9-year-old daughter, Liberty, stood weeping into the casket, having been denied a last visit with her mother.

Anna Antonio spent her last days making a dress for her 7-year-old daughter's birthday. When the girl received the dress, she expressed the hope that her mother's stay of execution would also be a present. Instead, Anna Antonio was executed on her daughter's birthday.

May Carey was executed just prior to her oldest son. Both were hanged on the same gallows. To the end her son put total blame on his mother, yet the two of them ate ice cream and cake together for their last meal, and he had comforted her during the lightning storm that preceded their execution.

Juanita "The Duchess" Spinelli, considered the "Fagin" of a small gang of thugs and described by Warden Clinton Duffy as "the only person I ever knew who could stand and talk about the weather while waiting to die,"[30] was executed in California's gas chamber with pictures of her children and grandson taped to her breast underneath her dress, which was her last request.

Elizabeth Duncan died alone in San Quentin's gas chamber. As she approached it, her last words were, "I'm innocent. Where's Frank?" Her son Frank, an attorney, was at that very moment pleading with the California Supreme Court to save his mother's life.

The simple answer to the question, "How many women have been executed in the United States?" is a numerical one. Thirty-nine during the twentieth century.

QUESTIONS FOR DISCUSSION

1. Why do you think more men than women have been executed?
2. To your way of thinking, would it be more difficult to sentence a woman to die? To execute a woman?
3. To what extent are women held more or less culpable in the criminal justice system?
4. Do you think the issue of gender equality has influenced the increasing number of women being executed?
5. Can you name the last two women executed in the United States? If you can't, is this an argument against deterrence?

THINGS TO DO OR SEE

1. Watch the movie *I Want to Live*, for which Susan Hayward received an Academy Award. As a class discuss whether on the basis of the information presented in this movie you believe Barbara Graham was guilty or innocent? Did she deserve the death penalty?
2. Watch the movie *The Last Dance*. Identify and discuss the issues raised by this movie. How realistic is it?

CHAPTER 3

PROCESS QUESTIONS

WHAT IS IT LIKE TO LIVE ON DEATH ROW?

My death row cell, my "house," was exactly ten feet long, six feet wide, and ten feet high. I measured it. What else did I have to do? When I got through measuring it, I paced it. When I got through pacing it, I counted 283 cinder blocks within my view, sixteen bars, and the only colors I could discern were white and some institutional shade of turquoise blue.

I am not a death row inmate, but for a brief while, one April afternoon, I became the fifth man on death row. My cell mates were four men awaiting their own executions. I knew when I would be leaving—they didn't. These four men had been here ranging from one to almost ten years. Eventually, one would die of old age, two by lethal injection, and one is still alive and appealing, after nineteen years—each of them spending from five to nineteen or more years living on the "row."

Over the previous several months I had been interviewing the men on death row about what it was like to live under a sentence of death. They had given me several accounts and descriptions but all had ended with, "If you really want to know, you have to be locked up out here." And, now, here I was— cell five, section C, death row. It is an actual place and only those awaiting death live here.

Eighty-Three Minutes

My stay on death row was only eighty-three minutes long—not quite an hour and a half. During that time I experienced, albeit to a very small degree, the loss of control, the boredom, the lack of privacy, the camaraderie, and the cuisine.

My meal was served by one of the death row inmates assigned as tierman. It consisted of a wheat roll, fifteen to eighteen carrot slices, two pear halves, a square of white cake with frosting, fried potatoes, a piece of fish, and milk or Sprite to drink. My cake was dry, potatoes too peppery, and the pears hard— otherwise it was not a bad meal.

Most of my time was spent taking notes as fast as possible. There was so much to experience and so little time to do it. I think, however, that my brief stay helped me understand what it is like to live on death row—at least what some of the issues and experiences are. The men told me, "Stay for forty-eight hours and you will have experienced death row—the rest is just a repetition—multiplied by years."

Since that brief experience I have spent over eighteen years interviewing the men on death row. Its composition and the faces—inmates and guards—have changed, but the same issues seem to remain. One official commented to me about my research on death row, "What do you want to study them for, they're just going to die." This attitude was common, but they don't just die. Many of them live there for sixteen to eighteen years. They are not the same people who did the atrocious killings. Some get college degrees, some find religion, some reach out to their victims' families. Many death rows are changing from actual places to a "death status"—wherein the condemned are no longer isolated and confined by themselves but are allowed to associate with each other and/or other maximum-security inmates. Sometimes programs and jobs are available to them. Whereas when executions were more "timely," there were no jobs or programming, now it takes the state many years to carry out an execution. Rather than the "land of the hopeless," some of these condemned inmates will be released—their sentences overturned or commuted, or they will be pardoned. Whereas, previously, there was only death on death row, now there is, if only infrequently, life—which gives hope.

There has generally been a great deal of curiosity about the death row experience and a fear and loathing of those who live there. Even in major prisons full of dangerous men, convicts stood aside as someone from death row was escorted through the yard to meet with an attorney or for medical reasons. It used to be such an escort was preceded with the shout of "dead man walking." Recently I walked the yard at San Quentin and watched everything come to a standstill as an inmate from death row was escorted. They no longer shout "dead man walking," but as they pass, armed guards step out onto the wall and the yard. All the inmates are required to turn their backs and face the wall. Those escorting the condemned, as well as the other guards, shout "escort."

Throughout my association and interviews with these men awaiting death, there have been several issues that seem to repeat themselves. These issues have to do with daily survival, relationships with each other and with the guards (and the "system"), living conditions and routine, and how they prepare to face death.

It is perhaps best if I let these men speak for themselves. The following quotes come from my notes and interviews with those who make their lives on death row and who will eventually leave to their deaths from death row.

Life on Death Row

Whenever I met with these men they were constantly troubled about the loss of control over their own lives. One man told me, "The only decision you have on death row is your decision to drop your appeals." Another man reflected,

"I've been in jail before but I've never been where I couldn't do anything for myself."

Some of these residents of death row get frustrated with the time it takes to get things done:

> When I first moved into this cell, my sink was clogged. It was not a major job to unclog it, but I had to ask for two days for a plunger to fix it.

He continued:

> I find myself getting tired of all the rules they have, especially on any incoming merchandise. It's frustrating trying to explain all the rules to someone on the outside before they can send you something. At times it seems easier to just give up and forfeit your privileges rather than conform to the rules.

This frustration, with the attendant loss of control, expresses itself further in their descriptions of the death row experience itself. One man told me he was glad to be there. "I was afraid I would get life. I can't do life, I can do death but I can't do life." Another commented, "The death penalty is a very cruel way of life." Another observed, "Death row ain't nothing but a slow death." This same inmate referred to death row as a "day care center."

While acknowledging that he probably belonged on death row, another man told me, "It's a good thing I'm here. Not for my sake, but for society's." He went on to describe his feelings:

> I tell everyone I'm doing OK but I really hate this place. The inactivity that is forced upon me seems almost unbearable sometimes.

Although at first life on death row appears to be a solitary experience, these men, because of changing conditions in modern prisons and because of their "status," still live in a social setting in which they interact with each other, staff, and other inmates not under sentences of death.

> What these guys do in here, in perhaps the final years of their life, is really private. It's really no one else's business. . . . I find them hard to talk with. They seem to have developed an effective protective shell around them and are unwilling to let just anyone in. It's like those on death row belong to an exclusive club and should be given respect as celebrities. . . . What is sad to me is the extensive publicity we get. I hated it myself, but what if some mixed-up kid decides he wants to become instantly well known? All he has to do is go out and kill, and if sex is involved, so much the better! The news media, of course, will

eat it up and dramatize it so that it can fill some sick need in people to know every gory detail. And then the kid will be punished for providing the entertainment.

Another, referring to some of his fellow condemned, commented:

They are proud of what they did. Think they are celebrities or something. I'm not proud of what I did—that there was something that wasn't planned to end that way—it was one of the hazards of [my] vocation.

This inmate was from the "old school" and felt uncomfortable around the younger residents on death row. He stated, "They're not criminals, they don't have a criminal mind—they're just stupid."

Most of these men have difficulty adjusting to their new punishment and their new associates:

If they can knock someone down that makes them feel better. My first six to eight weeks . . . I thought of ways to kill myself—then I would feel good for two or three days. I just wanted to crawl in my hole and lick my wounds.

Learning to deal with this requires quite a personal adjustment:

I've had to learn how to waste time since I've been here. You have to learn to take as much time as possible. When I eat I slow down. When I ate with a person outside who had been in prison he ate so slow— now I know why.

Hope is not totally absent from these men who are considered to be socially dead.

There might be a chance I might get off [death row] and I've tried to provide my own learning. I kept asking to talk to someone—at times—I would go into a rage in my head—I would ask to talk to someone but I guess they figured why talk to a dead man.

But hope is hard to sustain:

Up until now, it don't seem like I've been in prison. It hasn't been that bad. Now it's bad. If they execute me now it would be a relief. I've been fighting it all these years. I'm tired. Having hope and having it dashed, hope and dashed—that's the worst.

And yet each man has to find a way to cope with the experience in his own way:

> [Death row] is an extremely negative influence on me, and I constantly strive to contrive means with which to escape this place. . . . I hate waking up in the morning. I try to take a day at a time, but I hate the thought of beginning a new day. I suppose I "escape"—several hours each day—into a daydream fantasy world. I put on my headphones, turn off the cell light, close my eyes—thus shutting out both sight and sound of this place—and become a totally different person. In my mind I am a "good" somebody—a husband, father, boy, hero, etc.—*anybody* but a death row inmate.

Slight changes in schedule within such a confined environment can create problems for these men:

> You pretty soon get a schedule in here and you don't always want the schedule interrupted. If the schedule the prison has for us in here gets altered, we have planned our whole day around it and it really makes a difference when that happens.

There are cycles and stages these men inevitably experience. They describe and track them in various ways. On man monitored himself through the music binges he experienced:

> Watch . . . a person's attitudes, thoughts, changes—going backward and forward. I gauge mine by binges—the music I listen to—sacred music, jazzy music. I tend to have dreams in moody and sacred music phases. I'm always home . . . in my dreams. I deal with it by not worrying about anything I can't change.

He traced his development on death row for me by drawing this continuum:

__________\\

Came In   Last Few Years

Boneheadedness	Searching	Contemplated
(Anger and Hate)	(Read all kinds of books)	(Why I did what I did?)
		(Comparing my life)
		(Reasons; how I got here)

Another traced his own evolution:

> There are stages, ups and downs. Downs last longer than the ups. . . .
> Right now I'm not on one of my peaks—up for two or three weeks,
> down for one month. It's been this way ever since I came in—a con-
> stant—but now I have learned to deal with them better—my periods
> of doom and gloom. Usually somebody [on the row] is up and some
> are down. We've never been down all at the same time.

While they live with each other, they also live with the staff who are sometimes
referred to as the other residents of death row. Because of the intensity of these
constricted relationships, there is often a great deal of frustration and bitterness
on the part of the condemned:

> Staff was giving everyone a bad time. One time staff unplugged the
> TV right in the middle of a movie, just to harass us. They shine flash-
> lights right in our eyes at night, rattle the doors when we're asleep at
> night. Now they give us "psych" harassment. Or if you need some-
> thing done they just ignore the hell out of you. On the telephone, they
> act like they don't hear you when you ask to make a call or they don't
> bring it at the time you ask for it—or [they] will "accidentally" shut
> the phone off while you are calling or talking.

Another stated:

> Sometimes it takes days for a request to be responded to—and still
> more days before that request is filled, if it gets filled. I am getting to
> the point that I don't hope for things to happen. If I don't hope, then
> I won't be so frustrated and disappointed when things don't happen.
> Things don't happen more often than they do happen.

And further:

> I can feel anger and hate building up in me, especially against the
> prison administration and guards. One can't ask politely for some-
> thing in here and have it happen—he has to ask and remind and bug
> them again and again to have the request filled. I don't like anyone to
> have such complete control over me.

One of the men was a little more philosophical:

> There are no hard feelings on my part. I'm on one side and they're
> on the other. You can be a [prison official] and still be a human
> being.

Yet others felt they were getting the brunt of factors outside their control:

> Officers have different personalities and problems and they want to take them out on you.

And:

> I can't understand brutality and ignorance of the [officers and prison administration]—they could discuss and do things in a friendly, educated way.

The frustration and bitterness are not always one-sided. There was always, among the staff, the official and the "unofficial" rule book for keeping control of death row. One staff member told me:

> We have our ways of making these men do what we want—maybe not through the official way.

Such an attitude undoubtedly came after years of having to deal with men who have nothing to lose and who resent staff and other personnel who deal with them. One staff member about to retire told me that throughout his career he had dealt with three categories of inmates in maximum security—creeps, assholes, and maggots.

Although I encountered these attitudes early in my research, I noticed a change as those working on death row became better trained and educated. When I asked one staff member about his observations about working with the men on death row, he told me:

> One thing they all have in common is that they like to complain—about each other, showers, food, or whatever. This complaining isn't continuous though (thank goodness!). But if one starts they all join forces.

Such insight was not uncommon, nor was the attitude and experience of another worker who had previously assisted in the execution process:

> It's something ya have to do by statute but it's damned hard on us out here.

While our discussions centered mostly on their death row experience, my notes also record some of the comments by these condemned men about various other issues. These included:

CAPITAL PUNISHMENT
- We watch first-degree murder cases. If the person denies all through the trial, he gets the death penalty. But, if he admits it and says he is sorry, he doesn't get the death penalty.

- I didn't consider it a possibility of getting caught. . . . I considered it but I didn't think they would ever give it to me. The death penalty wasn't a deterrent to me. I didn't think I would get caught. The death penalty never occurred to me.
- I don't believe anybody has the right to take the life of another person—but since I've been here I met some people who don't deserve the right to live. Their sole purpose in life seems to be to make other people miserable. I could accept it if everyone who committed the same kind of crime I did would die.
- I've always believed in capital punishment. Provides catharsis to victims and society.
- I don't agree with what [other killers] did, but putting a bullet in his head [execution] doesn't teach us anything. Someone will come along next year and do it again and we won't know why.

CAUSES OF CRIME
- Competitive society breeds the potential for crime. Everybody loves a winner—success is measured by money—people get caught up in this. In doing so, they get involved in things they can't handle and end up killing somebody.
- Society produces crime. Every program on TV is about crime.
- It seems preordained that some people should die—silly reasons, accidents, and so on. Why? If I die, it was predetermined—as was the deaths of my victims.

TELEVISING EXECUTIONS
- Executions shouldn't be televised. It wouldn't shock the people—maybe for the first few executions, but after that it will become like Saturday night movies.

ORGAN DONATIONS
- [one of the men] got a letter from Dr. Kevorkian. He thinks we owe our organs to society. I would like to donate my organs but I don't believe I owe it to anybody. If they execute me, I feel I will have paid my full debt to society. My organs are extra. Anybody who gets my organs would probably be ashamed that they got them.

VICTIMS
- I was wondering about [one of the victims]. The other victims have recuperated to a certain extent—but he hasn't. It seems he just doesn't want to get better—he may enjoy the sympathy he received from the public—like he has been sitting around [all these years] waiting for me to die? Seems to me I am just an excuse, not the cause.

I can still remember that evening when I left death row. Eighty-three minutes—hardly a moment when compared to eighteen years of death row confinement. I figured I had barely "served" one minute for each year some of these men had been on death row. The smell was still on my clothes. Prison paint—be it battleship gray, army beige, or institutional white, cream, or turquoise—must have a smell. It saturates your clothing, sinks into your pores, and coats your nostrils. I remember the experience mostly by the smell—and by emotion.

I stepped outside, cleared the double secure fences, and took a deep breath. The air was cool, a slight breeze was blowing. Dark storm clouds were gathering over the mountains. I could hear the traffic from the freeway and, as I turned toward my car, I heard the crowing of a rooster pheasant filling its craw near the strip of "no man's land." None of this was being experienced by the men inside those walls—those 283 cinder blocks and sixteen bars.

It was at that moment I first realized that my research on corrections and death row is merely a professional "hobby" for me. I can't *really* understand because I can leave at will—returning to "my" world—as most researchers do. Life and death were going on behind me, and ahead of me was an evening of popcorn with my wife and children—a long way from death row.

QUESTIONS FOR DISCUSSION

1. What do you think would be the harsher punishment—execution or life in prison without hope of parole?
2. Could you live in a ten- by six-foot cell for twenty-three out of twenty-four hours?
3. Would it bother you to have to be totally dependant on someone else to meet your needs for food, exercise, and other physical needs?
4. How long could you exist in an environment in which you had no physical contact with another human being and you knew that every day brought you closer to death?
5. What is your definition of "cruel and unusual?" To what extent do you believe it applies to life on death row?

THINGS TO DO OR SEE

Lock yourself in your bathroom for forty-eight hours. You can take anything in with you that you wish—but you cannot leave or have visitors. Keep a journal—making entries at least two or three times an hour.

1. How long did you last?
2. What emotions did you experience?
3. What was the sequence of these emotions? Was there a pattern or cycle?
4. What did you miss the most?

HOW DO THEY SPEND THEIR LAST HOURS?

Something was obviously wrong. It was the morning of his execution and they had come for him, but he wasn't awake. They called his name, shook the door, but still no movement. In a panic they opened the door but it was too late—he was dead. They never found out where he got the pills. Some said it was a caseworker who slipped them to him. Others claimed his fellow inmates got them for him, and yet others believed he had saved them himself. Either way, he was dead. He had "cheated the hangman."

Removal to the Death Cell

It is to avoid this situation that, before most executions, there is a period of time—in some states twenty-four hours, in others as many as seventy-two hours—when the condemned inmate is removed from his regular cell and kept in isolation. This period of time is called the "death watch." Here he is kept under constant visual supervision. He is strip searched, given new clothing, and allowed no physical contact with anyone.

Three times I walked in the ritualistic procession from the cell house to the death cell. The last time was with an inmate who requested to be allowed to walk barefoot in the grass and to look up at the stars. As we started across the grass he began to laugh. When someone asked him why he was laughing he said, "I was just thinking how cool it would be if the automatic sprinklers came on and got all of you guys wet."

In many of those prisons where executions are conducted, the death watch cell is located only a few steps from the execution chamber. In Sing Sing and San Quentin it was often necessary for the condemned to walk right past the electric chair or the gas chamber—especially for women who were brought in from outside the prison. In such cases there was usually a canvas curtain or wall constructed so they would not be traumatized as they walked past it. Nevertheless, they spent their last hours only steps from where they would die.

It is during this period of the death watch that most of the rituals associated with executions take place—the last meal, the death watch log, and sometimes even composition of the last words.

Referring to the experience of waiting for death, and appropriate to the death watch experience, Dostoevsky wrote:

> But the chief and worst pain may not be in the bodily suffering but in one's knowing for certain that in an hour, and then in ten minutes, and then in half a minute, and then now, at the very moment, the soul will leave the body and that one will cease to be a man and that's bound to happen; the worst part of it is that it's certain.[1]

That is what the death watch experience is like. To know that you will die and exactly when that will be, and then, how to spend your last twenty-four hours?

The Death Watch and Log

I have spent the last eight to twelve hours with four different men who were executed. Each of them chose to spend those hours in a different way. Once each man enters the death cell, a log is kept at regular intervals. Known as the "death watch log," it documents the activities taking place, who enters and leaves the death watch, and any other observations—attitudes, emotional state, and so on—of the inmate. This log is then released to the press periodically during the last twenty-four hours in order to keep them informed of what is taking place and how things are proceeding. I have taken the following composite from actual death watch logs and my notes. I have combined them to protect the identities of those involved as well as to give an overall view of the last twenty-four hours of a condemned inmate. My notes and comments are in brackets.

Thursday [8:00 P.M.—Inmate is making final call to his mother. The escort team is waiting. He will be strip-searched, given a new jump suit, and shackled in preparation for removal to the death watch cell.]

Death watch log—9:00 P.M.—Inmate is now in the death watch cell. Cooperative during this operation. Time of arrival, 8:24 P.M.

[He stands by the door and looks around. Breathes a heavy sigh and begins to dress in the new clothes lying on the bed. Turns the water on, rinses his hands, washes out the sink, scrubs it clean—fastidiously. Is this an inmate ritual whenever they take over a new cell? A property ritual? Flushes toilet, wipes hands, sighs again, wiping his feet, sitting on the bed now, looking around. He puts the toilet paper in its place. General housekeeping. Makes his bed. Now putting on the coveralls. I look through the screened window and wave at him. He smiles and waves back in recognition. No one is saying anything. Not a word has been spoken.]

Death watch log—9:11 P.M.—Inmate has made his bed and is settling in.

[He is pacing his cell now—five paces and turn, five paces and turn, over and over. I am standing next to one of the death watch officers. There are two teams of four people each. They work eight-hour shifts and rotate each hour.]

Death watch log—9:30 P.M.—Inmate reading the Bible. Continued reading until 11:20 P.M. Went to bed at midnight.

[Nothing much going on. He continues pacing. Gave a sigh every once in a while. Rubbed his chin. Looked around. Picked up his Bible and began reading. One member of the death watch sits at the screened window and must constantly be looking at the inmate. Before him on a small shelf he keeps the death watch log, periodically making a note or an observation about the inmate's behavior or attitude. The inmate has gone to sleep now so I will leave and come back tomorrow.]

Death watch log—12:01 A.M.—Inmate is sleeping with a towel over his eyes to shade the light.

> 2:35 A.M.—Sleeping well. Has turned over two or three times but gone back to sleep.

> 3:27 A.M.—Inmate seems restless. Opened eyes, looked around. Still sleeping.

> 5:30 A.M.—Inmate is in the shower.

> 7:30 A.M.—Inmate refused breakfast. Stated he was fasting. Continues reading his Bible.

[During the day he met with his "spiritual advisor" and read letters he had received—some supportive and some antagonistic. He said he received the "usual" letter from Amnesty International, one from someone praying for him, and another congratulating him on finally doing the "right thing." At 4:05 P.M. I came back on the death watch. My presence, like any others coming onto the death watch, is duly noted.]

Death watch log—4:05 P.M.—Dr. Kay Gillespie arrives along with the psychologist. They talk with the inmate about his progress while in prison and his personal experiences.

> 6:00 P.M.—Dr. Gillespie leaves the room.

[As I talk to him I am curious as to how he is dealing with the fact that he will soon be dead. When I first visited him on death row, he told me of a recurring dream he had. He was in a small row boat, shackled, and with two prison guards. When they reached the middle of the lake he was pushed out of the boat. As he sank beneath the surface, he remembered the feeling—it wasn't unpleasant. He felt warm and comfortable. "I was transferred immediately to this big spacious house. I thought it was easy." He doesn't mention this dream now, but I can tell he is thinking about what is going to happen. He tells me, "I have this strange sensation that I'm being watched all the time—not the guards—but I felt some presence. I think they are ready for me on the other side." He continues, "It's a real funny feeling—tomorrow at this time I won't be here. I saw the birds when they brought me over. I thought, I'm going to miss you guys."]

Death watch log—7:05 P.M.—Inmate is quiet and appears to be doing well.

> 7:15 P.M.—Inmate comments about how well he is being treated.
>
> 7:30 P.M.—Warden enters. Inmate discusses the time the execution will take place.

[As the midnight time for the execution approaches, entries in the death watch log became more frequent. The warden's presence at this time is interesting. With the onset of lethal injection executions, the process has become more "sterile." The warden and other personnel seem to be keeping their distance. It used to be about this time on the last night that the "last meal" was eaten, often with the warden. Frequently, as well, the condemned inmate would order a large enough meal that he could give the leftovers to the other men on death row.]

The last meal is one of the most enduring of the rituals of execution. Perhaps stemming from Christ's Last Supper or some other tradition of last meals or last requests as expiation of guilt by those involved in the execution process, this last meal takes many forms.

- Prior to his execution, Timothy McVeigh requested and ate two pints of mint chocolate chip ice cream.
- In two of the executions I witnessed, both of the condemned decided to fast and requested no last meal.
- One inmate had a pizza, one wanted a Whopper, shake, and fries (plus Hubba Bubba grape bubble gum), and another ordered a banana split.

[With the increase of executions in Texas, the last meal has been limited by the administration to regular prison fare and specifically prohibiting bacon—it costs too much.]

Death watch log—8:00 P.M.—Inmate has not been informed yet by his attorneys but just received word the circuit court has denied a stay.

> 8:10 P.M.—Chaplain talking with inmate. They are praying together.

[The role of chaplain, spiritual advisor, priest, and so on seems to be crucial to the execution process—if not for the intended purpose of spiritual comfort, at least as a healthy distraction. It is the opiate of the death watch. Instead of focusing on the here and now, the condemned's attention is directed to the hereafter.]

Outside the death watch cell, unknown, unheard, and unseen, the execution chamber is being readied, the perimeter is being secured (including dogs and S.W.A.T. teams sweeping the area), and the executioners are being brought to the prison. Inside the death watch the process of religion continues.

Death watch log—9:00 P.M.—Chaplain is still here. They are singing some hymns, reading verses of scripture, praying.

> 9:27 P.M.—Psychologist and medical technician come onto the death watch. Asks inmate if he wants something to "take the edge off." Inmate declines.

[Each state and corrections system has its own policies and procedures (formal and informal) when it comes to sedatives or drugs prior to execution. Following the drinking orgies and "galas" of early England, it was later believed the condemned should be totally sober and undrugged so as to experience the full impact of the consequences for his or her behavior. More recently it has become acceptable in some jurisdictions to offer a mild sedative so as to ease the mind and body prior to execution. I'm not sure how much of this is out of concern for the condemned or how much to ease the process for the prison. One inmate told me it was somewhat ironic. He had been up all night awaiting his execution. If he took a sedative just prior to the execution, they would have to wake him up in order to execute him by putting him to sleep.]

Death watch log—10:30 P.M.—Inmate is talking to his attorneys.

[Frequently the condemned man's attorneys are the few people he knows best. They have probably spent more time with him than any other family or friends. Often he asks them to be present at his execution as his chosen witnesses. This last visit is usually to say good-bye and to tie up any loose ends—disposition of body, disposition of property, and so on. In some instances final papers to be signed have included exclusive rights to the condemned's life story or completion of a last will.]

Death watch log—11:10 P.M.—Attorneys leave. Inmate is becoming more agitated and restless.

[Those who work on the death watch become more intensely acquainted with the condemned than they did during their regular shifts on death row. One member of the death watch took me aside and confided in me. He said this experience had changed his attitude about capital punishment. "I used to be all gung-ho [for the death penalty] but now I'm not so sure. It would be easier if he [the condemned inmate] were a crud, but he is a nice, gentle person. I'm not sure we are doing the right thing by putting him to death."

I have had this same conversation on five different occasions— sometimes with prison staff, wardens, and even state officials who oversee the execution process. When I first observed the death watch experience, I was concerned the process had become too sterile. As the hours on the death watch passed, however, I observed a change in the relationship between the condemned and his death watch observers. They began to call him by his first name and would ask if he needed anything—even anticipating something prior to his request. It is perhaps this familiarity that leads to a self-assessment of one's role in the process.

This death watch experience seems to carry over after the execution. One supervisor told me the men who participated as members of the death watch seemed to have closer relationships with each other when they returned to their regular duties on death row. They seemed also to see the inmates, not just as "raw meat," but more as people. "They have more respect for life. The inmates are still inmates but the officers can better separate their crimes from them as people."

There are those who criticize the execution process as dehumanizing. If this is so—and I have not found it to be true—perhaps it appears to be so because those involved in the process must keep their distance, not to dehumanize the inmate or to sterilize the process but to protect their own human emotions as a result of their participation in this state ritual.]

Death watch log—11:30 P.M.—All visitors have left the death watch area. Inmate is in good spirits. Appears more relaxed.

> 11:45 P.M.—Inmate conversing with staff about World Series, politics, and taxes.

> 11:55 P.M.—Tie-down team enters death watch. Inmate is strip-searched and provided clean clothing. Remains calm.

> 11:58 P.M.—Inmate is restrained and removed from cell.

> 11:59 P.M.—Inmate exits with tie-down team and all leave death watch area.

Last Entry

Life as Usual—The Rest of the Prison

I remember thinking, as I was present on the death watch, that these men were counting down the hours to their deaths. The rest of the prison outside the death watch went on with business as usual. During this last twenty-four hours, the regular counts were held and called in to be sure every inmate was accounted for. Even this man in the death cell had to be counted, but his count was referred to as "minus one." From every aspect—outside the death watch—he was already a dead man. Inside the death watch, however, his presence, the presence of this one man, was the focus of all attention and activity. His every move was watched and documented. His needs and wants were attended to and, by some standards, he was in control and center stage. If only for twenty-four hours, he was "King for a Day." It is a very dubious distinction I'm sure. As stated in the punch line from a very old joke, quoting a man about to be executed, "If it weren't for the honor of the thing, I'd just as soon pass."

In retrospect I have tried to assess my presence during this death watch period. Sometimes I felt like an interloper, an eavesdropper, on a very private and personal experience. Other times I felt like I was a familiar face providing a personal connection on death row and a continuation of conversations begun but never finished. Sometimes, instead of my providing comfort, these men tried to make me more comfortable. They were facing death yet wanted to know how I was doing and if I was comfortable. I remember one of them asking me how I was holding up. I replied, "Not as good as you are." He laughed and apologized that I was stuck inside the death watch with him and missing all the activity outside the prison. When one of the men asked me what my exact role was, I told him I was documenting the process of the execution. He commented, "It must be pretty boring."

The death watch cell and the execution chamber have both been referred to as the "Dance Hall." Here, by folk wisdom, the men sweat and pace, rant and pray, plead and beg. None of this matches my experience. These men prepare for death with dignity and fatalism. They are, for the most part, aware of what they face yet choose to ignore their imminent death by sharing an interesting form of sociability with their tenders. There is a common bond formed by the circumstances of execution that makes both parties part of the ritual that is more symbolic than real. It has been this surrealism that remains with me. Did it happen? Was I really there? What has been accomplished?

QUESTIONS FOR DISCUSSION

1. What would you say to a man during his last twenty-four hours of life?
2. What would you choose for your last meal if given unlimited choice?
3. Could you actually eat a last meal?
4. What would be your last words?
5. Who would you want to invite to be present at your execution?
6. How would you spend your last twenty-four hours?

THINGS TO DO OR SEE

1. Write out a last statement, assuming you were about to be executed for a crime you did not commit; for a crime for which you were guilty.
2. See the movie *The Chamber.* Pay particular attention to the death watch scene.
3. Get a copy of *Dead Wrong*, a video made by John Evans prior to his execution in Alabama's electric chair. Do you think he achieved his goal? Do you think he was being sincere?

WHAT IS THE MOST "HUMANE" METHOD OF EXECUTION?

After leaving the death watch, I walked with him into the execution chamber—six members of the tie-down team, the condemned man, and me, walking that famous "last mile." He was cooperative as he helped them get him onto the gurney and, after he was strapped down, I watched as he removed his glasses and handed them to one of the members of the tie-down team. "I guess I won't be needing these anymore." Just as he said this I heard the red phone ring. There was a stay.

I am often asked if I believe the death penalty is cruel and unusual punishment. I'm not sure whether it is the actual dying that is cruel and unusual. Perhaps it is not the dying but the waiting to die. In 1941, Juanita Spinelli (The Duchess) stood outside San Quentin's gas chamber. Her execution was to be the first gas execution of a woman in California. She had received three reprieves and this time, as she prepared to enter the gas chamber, there had been another stay. It turned out to be brief and as Warden Duffy stood by her, he noticed the witnesses had not been reassembled. He asked her if she wanted to return to her cell but she said she would wait where she was. Warden Duffy remembered, "She was the only person I knew who could stand and talk about the weather while waiting to die."[2]

I watched as they unstrapped him and took him back to the death watch cell. I waited a while before going back. When I did, he was sitting on the bed, a blanket wrapped around his shoulders while he stared at the opposite wall. I chose not to intrude.

The stay lasted an hour. It was lifted and the countdown for the execution began again. My last glimpse of him was as he was again strapped down, IVs in place, as I walked through the execution chamber on my way to the witness area. Unable to raise his arms, he lifted his hands and wiggled them at me. "So long," he said and I replied, "Take care." While I waited as the other witnesses gathered, I could hear him talking with the warden. He appeared to be laughing. I later heard he had recommended, for the future, that pictures be placed on the ceiling above the gurney so the condemned would have something to look at while waiting. Maybe even pipe some music in like they did in the movie *Soylent Green*.

What method of execution would I choose? What is the most humane method of execution? Only in our modern society do we ask the question of "humane" ways of executing people. It is ironic that we would ask such a question.

Historically the execution process has intentionally been drawn out and painful. There is the familiar execution of Damien, for his attempted assassination of Louis XV:

> He was then laid on the scaffold, to which he was instantly tied, and soon afterwards fastened by two iron . . . fetters, one placed over his breast below his arms, and the other over his belly, just above his thighs. Then the executioner burnt his right hand (with which the villainous stab had been given) in flames of brimstone. . . . The executioner then proceeded to pinch his arms, thighs and breast, with red hot pinchers. . . . Then boiling oil, melted wax and rosin, and melted lead, were poured into all wounds, except those on the breast.

The executioner and his assistants proceeded to fasten round the criminal's arms, legs and thighs, the ropes with which the horses were to tear those limbs from his body. . . . When the cords were fixed, four stout, young, and vigorous horses continued their repeated efforts above the hour, without doing anything further towards the dismembering of the unhappy criminal, than stretching his joints to a prodigious length. . . . As soon as there was no appearance of life left, the trunk and dismembered quarters were thrown into a large blazing pile of wood, erected for that purpose near the scaffold, where they continued burning till seven o'clock the next morning and afterwards his ashes were, according to the sentence of the court of parliament, scattered in the air.[3]

Even this execution could be considered temperate when compared to some other methods used in the past. Among these have been:

beaten to death	crucifixion	pressed to death
boiled alive	drowning	sawn in half
broken on the wheel	flayed alive	stoned
buried alive	fried to death	strangulation
burned at the stake	impaled by stakes	suffocation

Some of the more creative methods of execution as documented in Geoffrey Abbott's book *The Book of Execution*[4] include:

Bastinado. "involved the victim's being caned gently and rhythmically with a lightweight stick on the soles of the feet . . . for many hours before the mental collapse and eventual death of the victim."[5]

Necklacing. "consists of placing a car tyre around the neck of a bound victim and setting it alight. The intense heat of the burning material, the fumes penetrating his lungs, and the effect of the molten rubber searing his body bring a slow and horrendous death."[6]

Spanish Donkey. "the torture consisted of seating the victim, his hands tied behind him, astride a wall, the top of which resembled an inverted 'V.' Weights were then attached to his ankles, these being slowly increased until the victim's body split into two."[7]

Cave of Roses. "method of execution in which the victim was confined in a cave which was already occupied by numerous snakes and poisonous reptiles."[8]

Over a Cannon's Muzzle. "The actual method of execution entailed the victim's being secured *across* the muzzle of a cannon or field gun, a shell then being fired, blasting its way through the victim's body and killing him outright."[9]

It is obvious that earlier forms of execution were intended to cause pain and suffering. These were often used as preludes to confessions and sometimes as expiation for the condemned's sins and crimes. With the advent of enlightenment and classical philosophies, attempts were made to reduce the types of offenses carrying the penalty of death as well as those methods used to implement it.

In the United States, five methods have predominantly been used for legal executions—hanging, firing squad, electric chair, gas chamber, and lethal injection. Each has been an attempt to take life in a more humane way. The history of punishment within the justice system, since the reformation, has been a history of good intentions. With few exceptions, the intent has been to improve conditions and to benefit the offender as well as society. The penitentiary was an improvement over hulks and the transportation system; the various methods of execution developed because of the intention to take life more quickly and, thus, more humanely. The evolution of hanging is a good example.

Hanging

Historically, hangings were actually strangulations. And, before that, they were hangings until the condemned was almost dead. Thus, it became necessary for the judge to sentence a person to be "hanged by the neck until dead" to ensure the sentence was completed rather than only one stage in the execution process.

After declaring a five-year moratorium on executions in 1969, the British government officially ended its use of capital punishment for murder. An execution chamber was still maintained in Wadsworth Prison in London, however, because the death penalty was still a possibility for treason.[10]

During ongoing debate to end the death penalty, the Royal Commission on Capital Punishment questioned the country's official public hangman, Albert Pierrepoint. He was sent twenty-three questions the Commission wished to have answered, and they then invited him to "comment on the merits of other methods of execution."[11]

When he made his appearance, and after establishing his credentials and background, the Royal Commission specifically asked him:

> do you consider that the method of execution by hanging as followed in this country is as humane and as quick as any method of capital punishment could be?[12]

Pierrepoint answered:

> Yes, I think it is quick, certain and humane. I think it is the fastest and quickest in the world, bar nothing.[13]

Syd Dernley, who worked as an assistant to Pierrepoint had a similar opinion, as he wrote in his autobiography:

> I hope I have laid to rest the myth that hanging was a barbaric form of capital punishment. The truth is that in the twenty years or so before its abolition in Britain, the system of putting a criminal to death had reached a degree of perfection that I believe is impossible to improve on. The execution was over so quickly that the condemned man could scarcely have registered what was happening to him; certainly he suffered no pain. To this day, I have yet to hear of any other place in the world where criminals are put to death more quickly. . . . Hanging was a merciful method of despatch.[14]

As a matter of fact, the process was so quick that it was once accomplished in seven seconds—an all-time record. So, not only was it quick, but, according to Pierrepoint, there was a secret to its efficiency:

> The knot is the secret of it, really. We have to put it on the left lower jaw and if we have it on that side, when he falls it finishes under the chin and throws the chin back; but if the knot is on the right hand side, it would finish up behind his neck and throw his neck forward, which would be strangulation. He might live on the rope for a quarter of an hour then.[15]

In actuality there was no "knot" in England. Pierrepoint explained:

> There is no knot. That fancy cowboy coil of a "hangman's knot" is something we abandoned to the Americans a hundred years ago. In Britain the rope runs free through a pear-shaped metal eye woven into the rope's end, and the operative part of the noose is covered with soft wash-leather.[16]

The actual description of death caused by hanging is reported as "causing instantaneous loss of consciousness. . . . As a result . . . the first, second and third cervical vertebrae are fractured or dislocated; the spinal cord is crushed or lacerated or torn from the brain stem, and if the initial shock is not fatal, the process is completed by strangulation."[17]

Pierrepoint's regimen was described by him as, "Cap, noose, pin, push, drop." By way of explanation he said, "Draw on the white cap, adjust the noose, whip out the safety pin, push the lever, drop."[18]

Hangings in the United States were not so scientific. Many were completed with a rope thrown over a tree or wagon tongue. Some states erected gallows and some had hanging rooms specifically constructed within the prison walls.

Wyoming and Utah added two interesting and unique innovations to the traditional gallows. Wyoming, out of deference for the feelings of the hangman, used a method of hanging developed by J. P. Julien and referred to as the Julien Gallows. It was first used in 1892 in Cheyenne to hang Charles E. Miller, 17 years old, who was sentenced to die because of his part in a double murder. Julien's contraption was referred to by some as a "Rube Goldbergism," and was described as follows:

> The mechanical arrangement of the gallows was very ingenious. Under the trap door was a post divided into three parts joined by hinges. The foot of the post rested in a socket containing a spiral spring.
>
> When the weight of the condemned man was on the trap it pushed the post down and an arm attached to the bottom opened a valve in a rubber hose which led to a bucket partly filled with water.
>
> The bucket was suspended to the arm of a lever on the other arm of which was suspended heavy weights to which was attached a cord which ran over pulleys to the post under the trap.
>
> As soon as the open valve allowed the water to escape from the bucket the lever which balanced the weights and the bucket of water tipped over, the weights slid from the arm and by means of the cord pulled the post from under the trap.
>
> The time to do this could be regulated almost to the second by the amount of water placed in the bucket.[19]

In essence, the man hung himself since he had to step onto the trap door to cause the water to start dripping. It has been suggested that some form of this device was also used in Colorado and Idaho. Apparently Mr. Julien never patented his device and it was not used after his death in 1932.

In Utah it was felt that a person could be more humanely hanged by being jerked up rather than dropped down. Charles Thiede was executed in 1896 for killing his wife in Sandy, Utah. Tried and convicted, he was given his choice of hanging or firing squad. He chose hanging and became the first and last to use this new method. The following picture illustrates the method:

The upward jerk apparently did not work very well for it took Thiede fourteen minutes to strangle to death. His neck was not broken. This method was never used again in Utah. The last remnant of this procedure that I can trace was when the weight was being used as a doorstop in the city/county court house in Salt Lake City as late as the early 1900s.

It seems to me that hanging would be one of my last choices.

Firing Squad

If I had to choose a method of execution, I believe I would choose the firing squad as being the fastest, most painless, and most humane—as well as being appropriate to the justice system.

In 1879, Wallace Wilkerson was executed by firing squad. His appeal to the U.S. Supreme Court was the first challenge based on the "cruel and unusual pun-

Charles Thiede hanged by being jerked upward rather than the traditional drop.
Salt Lake Herald. Reprinted by permission.

ishment" clause of the Eighth Amendment. He argued that the firing squad was cruel and unusual. In its ruling the court stated:

> Cruel and unusual punishments are forbidden by the Constitution, but the authorities referred to are quite sufficient to show that the punishment of shooting as a mode of executing the death penalty for the crime of murder in the first degree is not included in that category, within the meaning of the eighth amendment.[20]

In 1866, my great grandfather, John Gillespie, while sheriff, conducted one of the first firing squad executions in the state of Utah. As a child I read the description of this execution in his own words:

> Early in the morning, I pitched a small tent up on the bench, and had five men with rifles, four of them loaded with bullets and one loaded with powder, neither of the men knew who had the blank gun. I called out a company of calvary to keep back

the crowd of people, from all over the county. I set the prisoner on a chair about sixty yards from the mouth of the tent and covered his face and opened the front of the tent, and gave the word of command, and he was shot dead; we had his grave dug and buried him right there, and moved the tent and the men that night so that no one knew who did the shooting.[21]

Two things are particularly interesting to me. One is that this execution occurred only eight days after the crime and, two, the distance was sixty yards—180 feet! Today, the firing squad shoots from twenty-three feet.

Nevada, also, used the firing squad—sort of. There were two plans. The first one was to be done by a "squad" of three guards shooting rifles from a fixed position. Three rifles would be secured to a stand—one with a live round and the other two with blanks.[22] This plan was never carried out since the planned execution was stayed and the sentence commuted.

The second plan involved a machine consisting of three rifles clamped into a vise affixed to a wooden frame. A spot was to be marked on the back of the chair located 25 feet away. The rifles would be aimed at this mark and the condemned would be strapped into this chair. Three guards, chosen by drawing lots, would enter the room where this device was housed. Two of the rifles would be loaded and one would be blank. On command each guard would pull a trigger but they would do so without ever having to look at the man being executed. This device was used only once and that was for the execution of Andrew (Andreja) Mircovitch on May 14, 1913. The procedure apparently worked as planned. Newspapers reported Mircovitch walked unassisted to the chair and met his death bravely. Without a blindfold he looked squarely at the rifles that, according to the *Reno Evening Gazette*, sent "a leaden messenger of death through his heart, with an air of nonchalance."[23]

I was present at the last firing squad execution in 1996. John Albert Taylor, who chose the firing squad over lethal injection, stated he would rather die like a man than like a fish flopping around on a gurney. He told me, "It is symbolic to me. I maintain my innocence. If they put a bullet in me they are murdering me. It is the most hassle and the most expensive." He was executed for the rape and strangulation of an 11-year-old girl on the night before her twelfth birthday.

From fifteen feet away I watched as he was blindfolded and gave his last statement. Twenty-three feet in front of him stood five marksmen with five rifles resting on sandbags, peering through three long slits in the wall. I heard, "Ready—Aim— 1–2–3," and then one resounding bang. I had been given ear protectors but could clearly hear the discharge of the rifles—30-30 caliber. He lurched, his body straining at the straps. I saw his hands clench and unclench twice, then nothing. He was dressed in dark blue coveralls, but I saw no blood or anything else resembling what has been described as a "bloody spectacle." The entire procedure took four minutes and he was dead.

Firing squad execution chamber

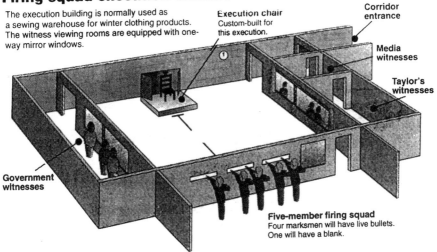

The execution building is normally used as a sewing warehouse for winter clothing products. The witness viewing rooms are equipped with one-way mirror windows.

Execution chair
Custom-built for this execution.

Corridor entrance

Media witnesses

Taylor's witnesses

Government witnesses

Five-member firing squad
Four marksmen will have live bullets. One will have a blank.

Firing squad procedure for execution of John Albert Taylor, 1996.
Standard-Examiner, Ogden, UT. Reprinted by permission.

As to the time it takes to die by firing squad, in 1938 Charles Deering allowed his heartbeat to be monitored by electrocardiograph throughout his firing squad execution. The prison physician, in an interview with *Argosy* magazine, indicated Deering's heart stopped beating 15.6 seconds after the bullets entered his body.

Although those involved with other methods of execution are generally professional executioners, those men who participate on the firing squad are not. In the state of Utah, they are volunteers from law enforcement agencies within the county where the crime occurred. Contrary to public perceptions, the state does not accept applications from the public in general, although whenever the media report a pending firing squad execution, the state receives a flurry of requests. One man wrote from Florida:

I was an expert rifleman in the military and continue to keep up my talent five days a week at the gun club. I can at 300 yards hit [my target]. I'll do it for nothing. You keep the $300 and give it to the . . . poor. I want the real bullit [sic] in my piece.

Another wrote:

Baby killers do not deserve to choose firing squad. Only proud men deserve to die by firing squad. Baby killers should die a pussy's death with lethal injection. [No] final cigarette. Just give them a Milky Way.

There are five rifles—four with live rounds, one without. The rifles are not locked into place but are held and aimed by living, breathing human beings. Twenty-three feet away they see another living, breathing human being whose life they must take. Although all five of these men are professional law enforcement personnel, and although none of them knows who has the blank round, each must deal with his participation in this process.

One member of the firing squad that executed Joe Hill in 1915 stated:

> It seemed like shooting an animal. How my thoughts wandered! It seemed an age waiting for the command to fire. And then, when it came from Hillstrom himself, I almost fell to my knees. We fired. I wanted to close my eyes, but they stared at the white paper heart, scorched and torn by four lead balls. Four blackened circles began to turn crimson, then a spurt and the paper heart was red.[24]

A member of a more recent firing squad interviewed for the *60 Minutes* television program by Dan Rather, when asked what he did immediately after firing, stated:

> After that I got the chills. I threw the gun down and cried, "My God, let's get the hell out of here." I was sick to my stomach. I heaved. I kept wondering if I was right. If I did the right thing. What right did I have being there. My God, I'd never do nothing like that again. I made that decision right then and there.[25]

Electric Chair

The accompanying picture represents the ideal process. Others describe the reality of death by electrocution as follows:

> In States which practice electrocution, the body of the condemned man is prepared beforehand with a fastening, and one of his pants legs is split in order that an electric plate can be placed against his leg. When the executioner throws the switch that propels the electric current through the body of the prisoner, the victim cringes from torture, his flesh swells and his skin stretches to a point of breaking. He defecates, he urinates, his tongue swells and his eyes pop out. In some cases his eyeballs rest on his cheeks; his flesh is burned and smells of cooked meat; sometimes a spiral of smoke rises from his head.[26]

In the late 1800s the age of electricity had arrived and cities and homes were experimenting with this new source of power. After observing an accident in which a drunken man touched an electric wire and was killed instantly, a dentist, Dr. Alfred Porter Southwick of Buffalo, New York, began experimentation on animals. He became convinced that he had discovered a more humane

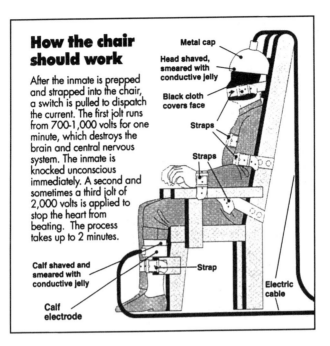

How the chair should work

After the inmate is prepped and strapped into the chair, a switch is pulled to dispatch the current. The first jolt runs from 700-1,000 volts for one minute, which destroys the brain and central nervous system. The inmate is knocked unconscious immediately. A second and sometimes a third jolt of 2,000 volts is applied to stop the heart from beating. The process takes up to 2 minutes.

Metal cap

Head shaved, smeared with conductive jelly

Black cloth covers face

Straps

Straps

Strap

Electric cable

Calf shaved and smeared with conductive jelly

Calf electrode

Procedure for execution in the electric chair.
The Orlando Sentinel/KRT. Reprinted by permission.

method of execution. His influence with the political powers of the state were evident when Governor David B. Hill, in his 1885 annual address to the legislature, stated:

> The present mode of executing criminals by hanging has come down to us from the dark ages and it may well be questioned whether the science of the present day cannot provide a means for taking the life of such as are condemned to die in a less barbarous manner.[27]

This use of "science of the present day" revealed itself in New York's decision to use "euthanasia by electricity" to execute its criminals.

The Electrical Execution Law became operational on January 1, 1889, and on August 6, 1890, William Kemmler became the first person to be legally executed by electricity. About having this "honor" Kemmler stated:

> I am ready to die by electricity. I am guilty and must be punished. I am ready to die. I am glad I am not going to be hung. I think it is much better to die by electricity than it is by hanging. It will not give me any pain.[28]

The execution took place at Auburn Prison and used George Westinghouse's alternating current. Thomas Edison had been approached for his advice on using electricity as a method of execution and had recommended the use of his competitor Westinghouse's alternating current. His strategy was that Westinghouse's current would, thus, become associated with death and danger, allowing Edison to market his direct current to the general population as a safe and useful current for everyday life.

Kemmler did not, according to all accounts, suffer a "painless" death. Westinghouse summed it up when he commented, "It has been a brutal affair. They could have done better with an axe."

Today the electric chair goes by several names—"Big Yellow Mama," "Old Sparky," "Old Smokey," "Gruesome Gertie," and so on—and we refer to the process as electrocution. At the time of its inception, however, there were other suggestions for such a death, including electromort, dynamort, ampermort, and electricide. My favorite was one proposal that would have referred to the condemned as having been "Westinghoused."

Some states have used "professional" executioners with technical knowledge about electricity. Robert Elliott served as executioner at Sing Sing and worked in other states as well. Other states have used some of their own personnel. When John Wayne Gacy was to be executed in Illinois, the state did not want its own people from the Department of Corrections performing executions. This opened the door to the possibility of using volunteer executioners and letters began to pour in:

- From a 73-year-old Mississippi resident. "Nothing would give me greater pleasure than pulling the switch on John Wayne Gacy, Jr."
- From a 42-year-old prison inmate. "I will soon . . . be appearing before the board of parole and I do need a job, plus a new start in life. I know a little about electricity, but then again, I am quick to learn."
- From a 38-year-old technician and "born again Christian." "I believe in capital punishment and look on this act as I do jury duty . . . realizing that everyone does not feel this way, I feel compelled to volunteer."

Other volunteers included a Baptist minister who, although not "thrilled at the prospect," would participate because "someone has to do it." One man from Australia said, although he would "feel no pleasure in killing," he would do it "for the money." And an Englishman volunteered because he admired the legal system, laws, and corrections system in the state.[29]

More recently, the use of the electric chair has come under criticism. Several "botched" executions have caused the public and the courts to revisit the use of electricity as an efficient and humane method of execution. (See Chapter 4 for more on botched executions.) Over 4,300 executions in twenty-six states have taken place in electric chairs across the United States since Kemmler died in 1890.

Many of these chairs now sit in museums or are boxed and stored in back rooms of prisons.

The gas chamber became the next innovation after the electric chair, and more recently lethal injection has become the most "humane" form of legally taking life.

Gas Chamber

While researching the history and use of the gas chamber I ran across the following article out of Phoenix, Arizona:

> **"DEATH KISS" AT EXECUTION PERILS MATE**
> Kisses pressed to the lips of her dead husband were blamed Friday night for the serious illness of Mrs. Frank Rascon, wife of the Mexican cowboy executed for murder early this morning.
>
> Frantic with grief, the woman threw herself upon her husband's body after the gas chamber was cleared of gas. Her kisses apparently contaminated her mouth with the deadly cyanide, which had killed Rascon, the sheriff's office said.
>
> A physician hurried to the Rascon home to administer aid.[30]

The use of the gas chamber has had an interesting history. While the continued use of this device as a form of execution continues to be debated, the chambers, themselves, stand as reminders of their use.

Three times I have stood in San Quentin's gas chamber, once even seated in Chair B. Never for an execution but only as a visitor. The hand-drawn diagram in my notes closely resembles the verbal diagram described by a reporter present at the 1992 execution of Robert Alton Harris—the last man executed by lethal gas.

> The viewing area is surprisingly confined, smaller than a two-car garage, with a ceiling twenty feet high. A dank, antiseptic smell is in the air. Shades are drawn over windows. The floor is green linoleum, the concrete walls are brown.
>
> Witnesses enter through an east door and across the room is the octagonal steel death chamber. Its interior is apple green and lighting seems to nearly glow in contrast to dim lighting in the witness area.
>
> The two steel chairs with their broad black straps are empty for the moment.
>
> More than fifty witnesses are present. They form two concentric circles. An inner group [official witnesses] . . . stands against a railing inches from the chamber glass. In the outer circle [are Harris's witnesses].

The use of gas for the purpose of execution, like other "new" methods, was introduced because, "It is contended by the advocates of this system that it is the most humane and merciful way of carrying out the sentence of death."[31] The

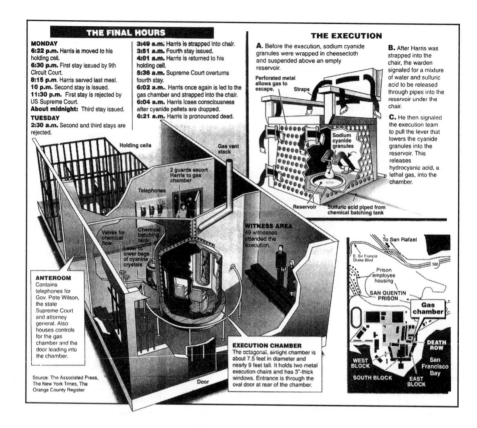

THE FINAL HOURS

MONDAY
6:22 p.m. Harris is moved to his holding cell.
6:30 p.m. First stay issued by 9th Circuit Court.
8:15 p.m. Harris served last meal.
10 p.m. Second stay is issued.
11:30 p.m. First stay is rejected by US Supreme Court.
About midnight: Third stay is issued.
TUESDAY
2:30 a.m. Second and third stays are rejected.

3:49 a.m. Harris is strapped into chair.
3:51 a.m. Fourth stay issued.
4:01 a.m. Harris is returned to his holding cell.
5:36 a.m. Supreme Court overturns fourth stay.
6:02 a.m. Harris once again is led to the gas chamber and strapped into the chair.
6:04 a.m. Harris loses consciousness after cyanide pellets are dropped.
6:21 a.m. Harris is pronounced dead.

THE EXECUTION

A. Before the execution, sodium cyanide granules were wrapped in cheesecloth and suspended above an empty reservoir.

Perforated metal allows gas to escape. Straps

Sodium cyanide granules

Reservoir   Sulfuric acid piped from chemical batching tank

B. After Harris was strapped into the chair, the warden signaled for a mixture of water and sulfuric acid to be released through pipes into the reservoir under the chair.

C. He then signaled the execution team to pull the lever that lowers the cyanide granules into the reservoir. This releases hydrocyanic acid, a lethal gas, into the chamber.

Holding cells   Gas vent stack

2 guards escort Harris to gas chamber

Telephones

Valves for chemical flow

Chemical batching tank

Lever to lower bags of cyanide crystals

ANTEROOM
Contains telephones for Gov. Pete Wilson, the state Supreme Court and attorney general. Also houses controls for the gas chamber and the door leading into the chamber.

WITNESS AREA
49 witnesses attended the execution.

EXECUTION CHAMBER
The octagonal, airtight chamber is about 7.5 feet in diameter and nearly 9 feet tall. It holds two metal execution chairs and has 3"-thick windows. Entrance is through the oval door at rear of the chamber.

Door

To San Rafael

E. Sir Francis Drake Blvd   580

Prison employee housing

SAN QUENTIN PRISON

Gas chamber

WEST BLOCK   DEATH ROW

SOUTH BLOCK   EAST BLOCK   San Francisco Bay

Source: The Associated Press, The New York Times, The Orange County Register

Procedure for execution in San Quentin's gas chamber.
The Orange County Register. Reprinted by permission.

state of Nevada was the first to introduce it and experts at the first lethal gas execution testified:

> Physicians and scientists who attended the execution were unanimous in pronouncing it a swift and painless method. Several of them said they thought it the most merciful form yet devised.[32]

The original plan called for the condemned to be executed while in his cell. Three tubes would open into each of the death row cells. Three guards would open each of the three valves, but only one tube would carry the lethal gas. Apparently this plan was intended to occur while the inmate was asleep in his cell.[33]

On March 16, 1921, the Nevada legislature passed a bill known as the "lethal gas" or "humane death" bill. By the time it was signed by the governor on March 28, 1921, it provided for a separate room to be constructed with airtight seals and thick windows. The lethal gas was still to be introduced while the condemned was asleep.

On February 8, 1924, Nevada's Gee Jon, the "Chinese tong slayer," became the first person in the United States executed by lethal gas. Prior to his execution, two appeals were made to the Supreme Court challenging the use of lethal gas as cruel and unusual punishment. The Supreme Court refused to hear both petitions.

As with other states that eventually used gas, the system was tried on animals first. Missouri referred to it as "doing the bunnies"; California used a pig. In Nevada, prior to Gee Jon's execution, two cats were put to death in the chamber to test its effectiveness.

Gee Jon apparently died quickly and painlessly according to most accounts. As to the method, a *New York Times* editorial commented:

> There is something peculiarly dreadful in the voluntary, cold-blooded killing of a man by putting him in a tightly closed room and letting in on him a poisonous gas.[34]

Other states soon adopted the use of gas. Most of them built "gas chambers." Some looked like diving bells, whereas others used varying shapes and sizes. Missouri's gas chamber was referred to as "the bottle." Wyoming's gas chamber still exists in the old abandoned territorial prison in Rawlins, Wyoming. It, too, resembles a "bottle."

Wyoming gas chamber—no longer in use.

In 1992, with the challenge to Robert Alton Harris's execution in California, Judge Marilyn Hall Potel ordered it to be videotaped, and she declared a moratorium on any further lethal gas executions in that state until she could rule on cruel and unusual issues. Other states subsequently called a moratorium on the use of gas.

Lethal Injection

There is a rumor on death row among inmates facing lethal injection execution. It goes like this:

> You are awake and aware. You feel everything—you just can't show anything!!!!

I am told that during some of the early lethal injection executions, the condemned man's legs would scissor on the gurney, so they started including muscle relaxants among the lethal drugs. I am also told some of those being executed by lethal injection would begin to snore after the first drug was introduced into their veins. Because this made the witnesses uncomfortable, they began including anti-snoring drugs into the lethal mixture. And now, I am told, there is the belief—based on anecdotal accounts from surgery patients—that the drugs only mask the outward manifestations of any physical reactions. I know none of this personally. It is only rumor.

I have personally witnessed five lethal injection executions and never have I seen any reactions or evidence of a struggle or discomfort. My issue with lethal injection as a method of execution has nothing to do with the method itself but more to do with its *symbolism*. It seems to me that death at the hands of the state, to fulfill the demands of justice, should have justice symbolism. I am not sure what that might be—perhaps hooded executioners, swords of justice, and so on—but not gurneys. The symbolism of lethal injection execution, as currently applied, is all medical—yet the medical establishment won't claim it. Sterile settings (including sterile needles), IVs, gurneys, and medical technicians all sound to me like preparation for surgery. It is an "operation" not an "execution." And, when completed, where is the sense of justice?

While on death row awaiting her execution, Pam Perillo commented on the irony of lethal injection:

> You know, it's strange but when I was out there using heroin all the time, I used to say, "I'm a hope-to-die dope fiend and when I die I'm going to die with a needle in my arm." And never did I even imagine I would end up in Texas where they kill you by lethal injection.[35]

Lethal injection is the latest in attempts to make capital punishment painless and humane. In Texas, on December 7, 1982, Charlie Brooks, Jr., became the first person executed by lethal injection. Eyewitness accounts state that Brooks:

> turned his head to the left and then to the right, then up again, and then to the left, as if to say "no." . . . His stomach heaved and after he had opened and closed his fists two or three times his fingers began to tremble.[36]

Sixteen months later on March 14, 1984, James Autry, in Texas, became the second person to die by lethal injection. His death, also witnessed by reporters, was described as follows:

> For the first five or six minutes he had no noticeable reaction to the solution. . . . Approximately ten minutes after the solution was started Autry had a subtle reaction to the solution. He rolled his head around, he opened and shut his eyes quickly like he was trying to stay awake. That seemed to pass. . . . Several minutes after that he seemed to roll his head around again and he shut his eyes for several seconds. His feet began to scissor on the Gurney and he seemed to move on the Gurney like he was trying to wrestle, trying to get out from under the straps. Shortly after that happened he closed his eyes again and they did not open. . . . He was pronounced dead at 12:40 am.[37]

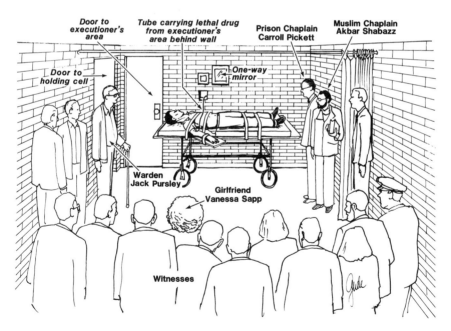

Depiction of Charlie Brooks' execution, the first lethal injection execution in the United States.
© Bettman/CORBIS. Reprinted by permission.

On its Web site, North Carolina has listed the equipment necessary to carry out a lethal injection execution:

COST OF EXECUTION SUPPLIES

12 each 60cc syringe @ .40 each	$ 4.80
6 each 10cc syringe @ .12 each	.72
3 each 1000 ml saline @ .71 each	2.13
3 each I-V tubing set @ .63	1.89
3 each I-V set (needle) @ 6.87 each	20.61
12 each I-V stopcock @ 1.23 each	14.76
4 each Thiopental sodium 5 gm. 100 ml @ 37.24	148.96
12 each Pavulon 5 ml @ 12.72	152.64
Total	$346.51[38]

The procedure generally consists of the administration of three or four specific drugs, depending on the state. First, a saline solution is started after the IVs have been inserted. There are two issues that arise at this point:

Issue One. Who inserts the IV? Generally medical technicians of some type attach the IV because the medical profession considers participation in an execution a violation of the Hippocratic oath and medical ethics.

Issue Two. Finding usable veins. Generally both arms are used in case one line gets plugged. Sometimes one line is inserted into the upper thigh (femoral artery). If there has been a past history of extensive drug use, the veins may have been collapsed and it may take extended time to find an appropriate vein.

Next, thiopental sodium is injected, which induces sleep and kills the brain. This is followed by procurium bromide (Pavulon), which stops the breathing, and potassium chloride, which stops the heart. There are two more issues at this point:

Issue One. The use of drugs as a means of execution was challenged in Texas and Oklahoma by death row inmates. They asked the U.S. Department of Health and Human Services to intervene because "there is strong evidence to believe [that the use of drugs] may actually result in agonizingly slow and painful deaths that are far more barbaric than those caused by the more traditional means of execution."[39]

Issue Two. Before the federal court, lethal injection was also challenged because "the Food and Drug Administration had not approved the drugs for the stated purpose."[40] They were not specifically approved for taking life!

It has not always gone smoothly. In some instances the condemned inmate, like Autry, had a reaction to the drugs—even gasping and vomiting. Sometimes the needle has popped out. Once the drugs were diluted by sabbateurs, and on one occasion in Texas, the mother of the man on the gurney jumped over the barrier and pulled the needles from her son's arms.

Lethal injection machines have been invented that automatically administer the drugs without human involvement or guilt. Some states still maintain "plausible deniability" by having two lines or buttons so those applying the drugs don't know who actually administered the fatal dose.

Lethal injection is now the most common method of execution in the United States. If, however, we have learned anything from history, it is that this method is only one of a continuing attempt to make executions less painful and more humane. Perhaps the future of capital punishment, if there is one, will develop methods of execution based on computers, space technology, or laser technologies. Perhaps even our perspectives and definitions of what is humane will change to accommodate our technologies. In a society where our realities are based on definitions, there are unlimited possibilities in the reality of capital punishment.

QUESTIONS FOR DISCUSSION

1. What innovations in the application of the death penalty do you envision for the future?
2. How would you prefer to be executed if you had to make a choice?
3. What method of execution do you believe would be the most humane?
4. What philosophical (theoretical) basis should be used in capital punishment. Pain? Revenge?
5. Given this theoretical basis, what form of execution would best meet the needs or be the most effective?

THINGS TO DO OR SEE

Watch the movie *The Green Mile.* Compare the electric chair procedure to the material presented in this chapter. What is the difference? Do you think it could actually happen as depicted in the movie?

WHAT HAPPENS TO THE BODY AFTER AN EXECUTION?

As I write, the ashes of Gary Gilmore are on my desk. On January 17, 1977, Gilmore's execution began the post-Furman generation of executions. Gilmore was sentenced to die for killing two young men in separate crimes. He was executed after he withdrew his appeals and challenged the state of Utah to "Just do it."

It was several years after the execution that I was visiting with Gary's uncle, Vern Damico. We discussed what led up to the killings, the execution that Damico had witnessed, and the aftermath, effects on the family, and so on. I asked if Vern had followed Gary's request that he be cremated and his ashes scattered over the nearby canyon. "Yes," he said, and then after a pause continued, "All but a handful—do you want it?" He then told me the remaining ashes were buried in a jar under a rosebush in his back yard. He dug it up for me and that is how they got onto my desk.

Policies vary from state to state and even prison to prison. Most states allow the family of the executed person to claim the body and conduct their own services. When the body is not claimed and the next of kin do not identify themselves, the inmate is buried at the expense of the state. Historically this has been done within the prison walls or in a separate area designated as a cemetery. More recently, in some states, the bodies are cremated and the ashes buried in a common grave.

Prior to his execution, November 19, 1915, Joe Hill wrote his last will in verse:

> *My will is easy to decide*
> *For there is nothing to divide*
> *My kin don't need to fuss and moan*
> *"Moss does not cling to a rolling stone."*
> *My body?—Oh—if I could choose*
> *I would to ashes it reduce*
> *And let the merry breezes blow*
> *My dust to where some flowers grow.*
> *Perhaps some fading flower then*
> *Would come to life and bloom again.*
> *This is my Last and Final Will.*
> *Good luck to all of you—*
>
> Joe Hill[41]

In addition to his last will, Hill made a last request to Bill Haywood, secretary of the Industrial Workers of the World (IWW or "Wobblies"). "Goodbye

Bill: I die like a true rebel. Don't waste any time mourning—organize. It is a hundred miles from here [the Utah State Prison] to Wyoming. Could you arrange to have my body hauled to the state line to be buried? I don't want to be found dead in Utah."[42]

Joe Hill (Joel Hillstrom or Haegland), a native of Sweden, was a nomadic poet and songwriter, who, as a member of the IWW, traveled throughout the United States singing his songs and rallying the immigrant workers to organize against the big labor bosses. He was executed in Utah for a crime that many believe he did not commit. (See Chapter 4.)

Bill Haywood did better than Wyoming. Joe Hill's body was taken to Chicago where it was cremated and a huge, emotional funeral held. A year later, on the anniversary of Hill's execution and at the IWW convention, Bill Haywood presented an envelope containing Joe's ashes to the delegates from many foreign countries and every state except Utah. He instructed them to "make the final distribution of these ashes with appropriate ceremonies when they returned to their respective homes and countries. By these means, the last will of Joe Hill will be carried out. The breezes will carry the dust to where some flowers grow, and they, revived and nourished, will bloom all the fairer, and the world will be that much brighter."[43]

It is interesting to note that one envelope apparently got sidetracked. It was discovered in the files of the National Archives in 1988. After this discovery, it was handed over to the IWW to decide what to do with them.[44] On November 15, 1992, this last envelope of ashes was scattered in Centralia, Washington, as a part of the Veteran's Day celebration. The location was the site of the 1919 lynching of a member of the IWW and the deaths of four other men as they attacked the IWW headquarters in Centralia.

With the advances in science and medicine in the early part of the twentieth century, it was inevitable that there would be attempts to bring the dead back to life and that this would spill over to the deaths of those who were executed. One of the more interesting examples of this involved the execution of Sam Salvatore Cardinella. Il Diablo (The Devil), also known as the "Murder King of Little Italy," was sentenced to be hanged for killing a man during the botched robbery of a delicatessen. But, to understand the sequence of events, we must first go back to the execution of Nicholas Viana who was a member of Sam Cardinella's gang. Viana, 18 years of age, was sentenced to be hanged for a murder very similar to that of Cardinella's—the murder committed during a robbery that netted him $6.50.

After a heart-wrenching farewell to his mother, he cursed Cardinella by stating, "Goodbye to all of you, except Sam Cardinella. May his soul be damned."[45] And, while standing on the trap door, he declared, "My last wish is that Sam Cardinella hang, too. He's responsible for me being here. He headed the gang."[46] Nicholas Viana was pronounced dead eighteen minutes later.

Viana's wish came true when Cardinella was hanged at exactly 10:26 A.M. on April 15, 1921, and pronounced dead at 10:34. He had left detailed instructions with his gang as to what was to be done with his body from that point on:

> He had arranged for his body to be claimed immediately after the hanging, and placed upon a hot water mattress in a casket lined with hot water bottles. The casket would be quickly loaded aboard an ambulance equipped with oxygen tanks and other life saving devices. It would be staffed with doctors and nurses ready to administer hypodermic injections, strap on the oxygen mask, and bring him back to life.[47]

Following the execution, as the ambulance containing Cardinella's body drove out of the prison yard, a guard became suspicious and alerted authorities. When stopped, the ambulance contained all of the equipment Cardinella had requested and was staffed with two doctors and a nurse. It was delayed for an hour after which, as rigor mortis began to set it, the doctor reexamined Cardinella's body to be sure he was dead. The ambulance was allowed to continue on its way.

It was later found out that this procedure had been previously attempted successfully on a hanged man—Nicholas Viana. Immediately following his execution, his body had been rushed to the ambulance—equipped as Cardinella had instructed for his death. In a room only a few blocks from where he was executed, Viana had been brought back to life:

> Within an hour, Viana's eyelids fluttered and a faint moan came from his lips. By all appearances, the experiment was a success.
>
> Viana, however, had been a traitor who had condemned Cardinella, his boss. By gangland standards, he was not worthy of the gift of life. The resuscitation was halted and he was permitted to die, once the rescue crew was satisfied that it could be done.[48]

Following Cardinella's attempted resuscitation, new policies required bodies of those executed to be held for an hour before the family could claim them and take them away. Such measures were taken because of a rather interesting complexity. According to one judge, there was the potential that once a person was pronounced dead after the execution, he was legally dead, and as such "if he was revived after being declared dead . . . he could go out and commit any crime that struck his fancy without fear of punishment, because, technically, a dead man is a non-person—and, thus, immune from the law."[49]

In 1928, it was rumored that such resuscitation efforts were planned for Ruth Snyder following her execution.

Ruth Snyder and Judd Gray were sentenced to die in Sing Sing's electric chair for killing Snyder's husband. The trial was a tremendous media event.

Both Snyder and Gray had 11-year-old daughters, and the public—especially men—became infatuated with Ruth. While on death row she received numerous proposals for marriage, and, prior to her execution, a petition was given to the warden signed by prison inmates who requested to take Ruth's place in the electric chair.

After her execution, it was discovered there had been a plan to resuscitate Snyder—if she could avoid the traditional autopsy. When interviewed after the execution, Warden Lewis E. Lawes admitted a rumor did exist that the electric chair did not actually kill but only stunned and that the real cause of death was the autopsy. He explained that, for that reason, he had ordered there be one long sustained shock rather than the several short ones that were usually administered.[50]

One of Snyder's attorneys, Joseph Lonardo, admitted there had been a plan to revive Mrs. Snyder. They had hoped to obtain her body immediately after the execution and to administer adrenalin injections to restore her to life. Her attorney filed a last-minute appeal "commanding" the warden to not authorize an autopsy. It had been signed by Josephine Brown, Ruth's mother. The warden refused this appeal, the autopsy was held, and Ruth Snyder is still dead.

QUESTIONS FOR DISCUSSION

1. What do you believe should be done with the bodies of those executed? Should they be available for public display? Would it help deter other criminals?
2. Should autopsies be performed as a matter of policy?
3. Are there things that could be learned by studying the bodies (brains, tissues, genes, etc.) of those executed? What are they?
4. Is it realistic to think that someone could be resuscitated after an execution? Should this be a concern of prison officials? Would it change the legal status of the one resuscitated?
5. If a person, after execution, is found to still be alive, should he or she be pardoned and released or executed again until dead?

THINGS TO DO OR SEE

1. Go to a cemetery and try to locate the grave of someone who has been executed. Is the grave located in the "good" or "bad" section of the cemetery?
2. Visit a prison cemetery. Are the graves marked with names or numbers?

Reprinted with special permission of North American Syndicate.

WHO DOES THE EXECUTING AND
WHY ISN'T IT PUBLIC?

I have walked the route from where London's Newgate Prison once stood (now the site of the Old Bailey) to the site of the Tyburn Gallows—the old triple tree—on Edgeware Road, near the present Marble Arch. As I walked along this modern thoroughfare with names such as Newgate, Holborn, and Oxford (originally Tyburn Road) Streets, through the present districts of Holborn, St. Giles, Soho, and Mayfair, I envisioned the spectacle of those days of public executions.

The trip that was over two miles long began at Newgate Prison with the bell of St. Sepulchre tolling out the hours and black flags draped along the route "celebrating" the execution. The condemned, and his or her coffin in the back of the cart, made slow progress—sometimes taking two to three hours—depending on how many stops were made. The crowd would be simultaneously cheering and jeering; the condemned toasting the crowd as the process made stops at various pubs, including the Bowl with its corner location at St. Giles High Street and in Holborn at the George.[51]

Rather than perceived as rogues or outcasts, those on their way to Tyburn received sympathy, even respect, as they posed with bravado and good humor. By custom their dress was often formal, men in traditional garb, women in gowns. One woman even wore her wedding dress. Each was expected to address the crowd, which often numbered in the thousands. Some of the spectators had even reserved bleacher seats or window boxes. These last speeches were intended to allow the condemned an opportunity to confess but were, more commonly, used for extended braggadocio to further enhance the condemned's reputation for approaching death without fear. Actually, this last speech provided an opportunity to denigrate the court and its officials.

The spectacle of public executions no longer exists in the United States. It was believed, at the time, that those who witnessed these public executions would learn about the consequences and be deterred in their future behavior. In reality, these occasions were used by pickpockets and other criminals to practice their profession on the large crowds gathered for the event. Rather than providing the somber, reflective atmosphere intended, these public executions became occasions for public drunkeness, celebration (see "gala," Chapter 2), and even riots. Boos and catcalls often attended the actions of the executioner and the "performance" of the condemned was often either cheered or derided.

England's last public execution took place in 1868 by hanging, France's in 1939 by guillotine, and in the United States the last public execution was a hanging in Missouri in 1937. There are, however, other countries that still continue the practice of public executions. In China the condemned is publicly shot in the back of the head while kneeling. Around the neck is a sign describing the crime. Saudi Arabia uses public beheading, Nigeria and Iran use the firing squad in the public square, and Afghanistan still uses public hanging.

In some Islamic countries, not only are public executions conducted, but the victims' families are also allowed to actually participate in the execution. News reports out of Afghanistan describe executions carried out by family members:

AFGHANISTAN: VICTIMS' RELATIVES EXECUTE KILLERS

Peshawar, Pakistan—As a crowd of thousands looked on, the relatives of two murder victims ignored pleas for mercy and executed the convicted killers, as some believe is decreed by Islamic law. . . . Armed guards led Mohammed and Ullah, both blindfolded, into the square and stood them up against a large tree. "It is my right to do this," said Sharif Khan, the uncle of one of the murdered men. "It was a fair trial and I want justice." Khan aimed his automatic rifle at Mohammed and fired more than a dozen bullets. When Mohammed moved slightly, Khan let loose another burst of fire. The father of the second victim shot and killed Ullah with four bullets aimed at the head, witnesses said.[52]

HUSBAND EXECUTES MAN WHO KILLED HIS WIFE

Kabul, Afghanistan—Shielding his face in fear, a convicted murderer crumpled to the ground in a burst of automatic gunfire—shot by the husband of the pregnant woman he killed. A thousand people gathered . . . to watch justice in Afghanistan's capital, Taliban-style. . . . [I]t was the first [execution] under the new rulers' strict version of Islamic legal process, which includes victim retribution. Under a cloud-filtered winter sun, Mohammed Alif knelt and took aim at the 30-year-old killer of his pregnant wife and their three children. Ghulam Mahmad lifted his arms against the spray of bullets. Standing over his prone body, Alif fired a second burst.[53]

There is an ongoing debate in the United States as to whether public executions should be brought back. Some of those who support such a process come from both sides of the capital punishment debate. By supporting public executions, the proponents of capital punishment argue, the observation of an execution would certainly serve as a deterrent. At the same time, those who would abolish capital punishment argue for public executions because the spectacle, they believe, would be so traumatic there would be a public outcry to do away with the death penalty.

Although most experts see little chance that public executions will return to this country, there are still debate and lobbying to at least provide for the televising of executions. This movement is led particularly by the media and television industry. Such an occurrence actually happened in Italy. In 1992, an Italian television program *Television Encounters* broadcast what was claimed to be the execution of a U.S. inmate. The execution was apparently secretly filmed by a freelance reporter in a prison somewhere in the midwestern United States.[54] Even the Vatican was incensed over this departure from good taste.

The debate about televised executions came to a head as the execution of Timothy McVeigh became a reality. Over a thousand family members of victims from the explosion at the Murrah Federal Building were eligible to view the execution. At the newly built execution facility at Terre Haute, however, there was room for only ten victims' family witnesses. These places would go to those selected by a random draw. To accommodate the others, it was decided to provide a closed-circuit television broadcast of the actual execution.

As could be expected, this decision fanned the flames of the debate over public and televised executions. Arguing the case in favor, reporter Tony Mauro wrote in *USA Today:*

[A]t least some of us would have preferred that today's execution of Oklahoma bomber Timothy McVeigh had been televised. . . . Executions, whether you approve or not, are among the most important acts of government—your tax dollars at work. Especially in the context of an issue that divides the public, every aspect of capital punishment, including the ultimate act, should be subject to as much public scrutiny as possible. . . . Under our justice system, crimes are viewed as an offense to society in general, not just the specific victims who have been harmed. If the victims of the Oklahoma City bombings could witness the execution via closed-circuit television, then society in general is just as entitled.[55]

Taking an opposing view, author Jonathan Kellerman wrote:

The Murrah families deserved to watch McVeigh take his last breath. . . . The families also earned the right to go through an emotionally wrenching event in private. By turning McVeigh's final moments into a public spectacle, we would have diluted their experience and engaged in the worst type of emotional pretentiousness—the facile big lie of I-know-what-you're-going-through. It would have robbed them of their dignity.[56]

Famous photo of Ruth Snyder's execution captured at the moment of execution by a hidden camera. New York Daily News. Reprinted by permission.

For the most part, cameras and recording devices are not allowed in the execution chamber. Certainly the events of January 12, 1928, when Ruth Snyder was secretly photographed as the switch was thrown on "Old Sparky," intensified all efforts to keep executions from public view.

Recently some old audiotapes were discovered in Missouri. These recordings were made of executions conducted by the state and contained the voices of those involved in each execution as well as sounds of the execution itself. The tapes were made for the purpose of documentation and training but, when discovered, were broadcast over public radio.

Also, in 1992, by order of U.S. District Judge Marilyn Hall Patel, the gas chamber execution of Robert Alton Harris in California was videotaped and then sealed to be used as evidence should there be any litigation in the future as to whether execution by gas was to be considered cruel and unusual.

With few exceptions, as noted earlier, executions in this country occur within the walls of prisons and are conducted by state officials, witnessed by legislatively controlled officials, and reported through approved media representatives, all of whom have been thoroughly searched and are constantly monitored.

Although some countries maintain the concept of "victim retribution," others that have historically used capital punishment have institutionalized the role of executioner. In France, the Sanson family served as state executioners for

THE FAR SIDE® By GARY LARSON

Mobile hobbyists

almost 200 years. As a rule, the public executioner was given no salary but was, as an accommodation, allowed a tax. He would send his assistants to collect it, which consisted of:

> an egg from each basket, a fruit or a bunch of grapes from each crate, a small or large fish from each barrel, a handful of vegetables from each crate put on sale . . . a *sou* from each barrow unloaded, two *sou* for a one-horse cart [and] twice that amount for a cart and pair.[57]

In collecting these taxes, the executioner's assistants were often rather aggressive, thus giving rise to the expression "as insolent as an executioner's assistant."[58]

The Sanson family used as a crest a cracked bell, suggested by some to be a play on words *sans son*, meaning "no sound."[59] Six generations of Sansons plied their trade as French executioners in which they presided over the executions of such notables as Louis XVI, Marie Antoinette, Robespierre, Lesurques, Cadaudaul, and Louvel.[60]

For a period of time the Sansons, as public executioners, wore a uniform with the mark of a ladder and a gibbet when performing their duties. For a while they were allowed to remove this symbol, which they considered a mark of shame, but eventually returned to the traditional uniform that consisted of "blue breeches, red jacket with a gibbet and a ladder embroidered in black."[61] It was this uniform that they wore to the famous execution of Damiens who had made a feeble attempt to kill the king. As described in Chapter 3, his punishment dictated by the "Parlement" included having the offending hand that held the knife burned with sulphur, the flesh from the chest and thighs torn with pincers, molten lead poured into his open wounds, and then eventually being pulled apart by four horses, each going in a different direction. Ironically, one of the four horses fainted.

The family apparently experienced various forms of humiliation and shame as a result of their occupation. People shunned them, other children were not allowed to play with theirs, and they were even excluded from other occupations. Charles-Henri Sanson, when appearing before the "Parlement," made an attempt to have them understand his plight:

> Ask a soldier what his profession is and he'll reply, as I do, that he's a slayer of men. But that has never made people think of avoiding his company, and nobody considers it a dishonor to eat with him! And who does this soldier kill? Innocent people, people who are only doing their duty. . . . While I, in the exercise of my functions, respect the innocent and only deal out the death of the guilty; I only purge society of the villains disturbing the peace.[62]

The executioners of France were not the only ones to feel excluded from "decent" society because of their profession. England's hangmen also felt and were treated similarly.

Because of the notorious John Catch or "Ketch" who became England's hangman in 1663, subsequent hangmen became known as "Jack Ketch." Children were made to behave with the threat, "Jack Ketch will get you."[63] And, it was Jack Ketch "more than anyone else [who] was responsible for establishing the public executioner in modern times as a rogue character to be shunned by respectable society."[64]

To assist the hangman, other criminals were pressed into service as were chimney sweeps in some parts of Scotland. It was not unusual for men, under sentences of death, to receive commutations if they would agree to serve as executioners. Women under sentences of death could receive commutation by marrying the hangman.

In England, in contrast to France, public hangmen generally had to apply for the job. The role did sometimes pass from father to son—or at least stay in the family—but it was not a hereditary role.

Albert Pierrepoint, England's last hangman, followed in the footsteps of his father Henry (called Harry) and his Uncle Thomas. Albert became one of the most famous hangmen in England and served over one of the longest periods from 1931 to 1956. He applied to the Home Secretary at age 25 and began working with his Uncle Tom at age 27. He was the last of a long line of men who served the government in this capacity. Most came from backgrounds as tinkers, barbers, cobblers, and so on. Their patron saint, at first, was St. Crispian, patron saint of cobblers and shoemakers. Later they adopted St. Constantine and St. Helen, patron saints of barbering.[65]

It is often assumed that these men suffered nightmares and apparitions. Pierrepoint claimed to never have experienced such ghosts but some of his colleagues admitted to various degrees of haunting, delusions, and illnesses.

After retiring as hangman in 1824, Jeremy Botting sustained lingering illness and apparently the suffering increased in his later years as he was "much troubled by the ghosts of all those he killed."[66] In 1888, after James Berry hanged three men in Ireland, "he suffered a mild nervous breakdown and took some weeks to recover."[67] Following his retirement, hangman John Ellis, after a failed attempt at suicide by shooting himself in the head, finally succeeded, in 1932, when he cut his own throat with a razor. His family said he suffered from insomnia and depression as a result of the men he had executed but especially because of the two women he executed.

Many of these men turned to drink in order to assuage their inner turmoil and emotions. John Robert Radclive, a Canadian hangman, is said to have consumed a bottle of bourbon after each execution he conducted:

> He would toss about in a cell or a small room in the prison until it was time to catch his train. With him in the dark, he claimed, were the ghosts of all those he had hanged, his own private chamber of horrors.[68]

Radclive also claimed that, because of his profession, his family deserted him and changed their names.

Such a profession carried with it many consequences, not only for the hangman but also for his family. William Calcraft was ostracized by his neighbors and would leave his home in the night so as not to attract their attention. James Berry's wife, who suffered the same ostracism as her husband, had to work hard to protect her children from the same negative consequences. John Ellis reported:

> Conversations cease suddenly when I am about . . . and I can feel people eyeing me as if I am some exhibit in the chamber of horrors. They will avoid shaking hands with me when introduced—they shudder at the idea of grasping the hand that has pinioned murderers and worked the gallows lever. Socially it is a bad business being a hangman.[69]

There were other consequences for executioners. In Nürnberg, Germany, the executioner was not allowed to live within the city limits. His house can still be seen suspended over the Pegnitz River. In some countries:

Daughters of executioners were forbidden to marry men outside the profession, and communities sometimes decreed that executioners' houses had to be painted red. Merchants frequently refused to sell goods to executioners, fearing that other customers would be frightened away. Even an executioner's donkey was cropped and marked so people would know that it belonged to the hangman.[70]

Some of these men, it was claimed, were able to rise above any pejorative effects. One of these was William Marwood, known as the "gentleman executioner." He insisted he was an *executioner* and not a *hangman*, and to some:

he was thought of as a family friend, a benefactor of mankind. There was nothing of the recluse about him. He wore the term "social pariah" with a difference. His appearance was respectable, his dress and grooming never at a loss. And, while his fellow townsmen told jokes about him, such jokes savored of good humor rather than dislike or repulsion.[71]

Syd Dernley, a contemporary of Albert Pierrepoint, felt a great deal of pride in his experience and association as a hangman:

The men who operate the gallows were, like the system, the best in the world, and I am proud to count myself in their number. We were, apart from being hangmen, very ordinary people, a ragbag collection of individuals. . . . Most were family men and most were moderately successful in their lives away from the execution chamber.[72]

Others of these men, however, were not as complimentary as Dernley of their chosen profession. James Berry confessed to having a "heavy conscience" and believed his chosen career had been "ill considered":

I now hold . . . that the law of capital punishment falls with terrible weight upon the hangman and to allow a man to follow such an occupation is doing him a deadly wrong.[73]

Many of these men turned to religion in their later years, some even denouncing capital punishment after their careers came to an end. James Berry was one of these who even went on the lecture circuit to speak about its evils. Dernley, on the other hand, never experienced such a change of attitude. Referring to Berry's new conversion, Dernley commented, "When you have hanged more than 680 people, it's a hell of a time to find out you do not believe capital punishment achieves anything."[74]

In addressing the religious conversion of some of his colleagues, Dernley commented:

There have been many executioners in history who turned to religion late in their lives when their hanging days were over. . . . [B]ut that never happened to me. . . . I do not expect to come face to face with any of our clients again.[75]

Pierrepoint, on the other hand, believed his role as executioner to be a calling. "I have always believed that I received a call to become an executioner, just as I was guided when I gave up the vocation."[76] He, too, became disenchanted with the concept of capital punishment and its application:

> The fruit of my experience has this bitter after-taste: that I do not now believe that any one of the hundreds of executions I carried out has in any way acted as a deterrent against future murder. Capital punishment, in my view, achieved nothing except revenge.[77]

None of these executioners seemed to be particularly bothered by the guilt or innocence of their victims. Berry is said to have slept better after those executions in which the condemned had confessed on the way to the scaffold. Part of this peace was a result of his often stated belief, "They don't tell lies to the hangman."[78]

Incidentally, it was this belief that caused Berry to believe he had actually hanged Jack the Ripper. It was suggested to him by Scotland Yard that the man he was about to hang, William Henry Bury, was under investigation as a possible suspect in the Jack the Ripper murders. They asked Berry if he would quiz and probe a little to see if he could get any information out of Bury. In the process of doing this, Bury apparently said to Berry, "I suppose you think you are clever to hang *me*, but you are not going to get anything out of me." Berry claimed the investigators agreed there was something significant in Bury's emphasis on *me*, which would indicate he was more than just a wife murderer. Berry remained convinced throughout his career that he had hanged Jack the Ripper.[79]

Other executioners also found some relief in hearing confessions—supposedly because of personal concerns about executing an innocent person. As previously quoted, Helmi Sultan, the Egyptian state executioner, benefited from such confessions:

> What makes me feel psychologically good is when I am putting the rope around the convict's neck, I hear him muttering his last words: "Forgive me God. Forgive me God." These words indicate he is guilty.[80]

Robert Elliott, probably the best-known executioner in the United States, had similar concerns about the guilt or innocence of those over whose executions he presided:

> Nothing in the death chamber disturbs me more than to hear a person with only a few seconds to live insist that justice has erred. When this occurs, my steps from the chair to the controls are slower than usual. My hand seems to hesitate on the switch. Greater effort is necessary to perform the execution.[81]

Robert Elliott was selected as official executioner upon the recommendation of Sing Sing's Warden Lewis Lawes in 1926. Prior to that he had assisted Edwin F. Davis (who supervised the construction of the first electric chair) and then John Hulbert, both of whom served as executioners for the State of New York. Elliott replaced Hulbert who resigned his position and eventually committed suicide in the basement of his own home. In his memoirs, Elliott claimed to have executed 382 men and five women.

The United States has not had the lengthy history of capital punishment that England has or the generations of executioners. However, the career of Robert Elliott presents the unique history of the United States with regard to its own unique method of execution—the electric chair.

Elliott, who worked his way through the system as an electrician in the prison system from Dannemora, Auburn, and then to Sing Sing, was a natural to assume the role of executioner. After assisting Davis on many occasions, he was appointed officially as executioner at Sing Sing but also conducted electric chair executions in New York, New Jersey, Connecticut, Pennsylvania, Massachusetts, and Vermont. His experience and reputation paralleled that of his English colleagues:

Avoided and ostracized: I have been, intentionally or otherwise, painted as some kind of ogre. Even pictures of me have been retouched so I would resemble something akin to the loathsome Mr. Hyde. After reading many of the distorted descriptions of me and my work, I can readily understand the popular impression that people run for cover when I walk down the street; that I live a very unnatural life, and that my family and I are lonely and friendless.[82]

Routine after execution: Upon finishing my work, I leave the prison. I feel as though a great burden has been lifted from me, for I never permit myself to relax for a second during an execution. If I am at either Ossing or Trenton, I return home immediately. In the other cities, I spend the rest of the night at a hotel, departing . . . early the next day.[83]

Concern for the condemned: Then I throw the switch. As I do so, I often pray silently, May God have mercy on your soul.[84]

Opposition to capital punishment: It is generally assumed that, because of my occupation, I am in favor of capital punishment. I do not think that the death penalty is necessary to protect society, and do not believe that it should be inflicted. When I first entered the work, I had no particular views on the subject; but reached my conclusions after being official executioner for a number of years.[85]

Conclusion

Over time, the execution process has changed dramatically. The "gilded age" of executioners who were involved in the process has, in a sordid sort of way, been altered. Earlier, a rather "intimate" relationship existed between the hangman and his victim. Berry described it as:

> a bond [that] connected the hangman and his victim. . . . They were each dependent upon the other: the hangman for the victim's cooperation and steadiness, the victim upon the executioner's skill and speed.[86]

Pierrepoint believed this relationship served an important role in the efficiency of the execution itself:

> I had to inspire the maximum confidence in the other participant in the drama. A "drama" is no idle word. . . . The swift but measured course of events which leads to the humane killing of a man demands rehearsed competency and unquavering [sic] confidence from all concerned . . . including the condemned man.[87]

Whereas earlier executioners wore masks and hoods, in England executioners were well known, sometimes even cheered and applauded. Some of them owned or worked at pubs and other public businesses. Ellis hosted at "The Jolly Butcher" pub; Pierrepoint owned two pubs, at different times, "Help the Poor Struggler" and the "Rose and Crown"; Calcraft could be found at the "Tiger" and wore a flower in his lapel; and, as previously mentioned, Marwood, the "gentleman executioner," could be identified by his coat and tails and his felt hat, which he tipped to ladies as he passed them on the street.

Then, particularly in the United States, things began to change. Robert Elliott attempted unsuccessfully to keep his identity secret. Other executioners, for the most part, remained hidden and anonymous in this country. Not only were their identities protected, so too was the extent to which personal responsibility could be attached to them or others involved in the process.

Whereas earlier there was the shaking of the hangman's hand by the victim, it was also customary for the hangman to ask (and receive) the victim's forgiveness for what he was about to do. As capital punishment progressed in the United States, various procedures and methods of execution were developed to distance the executioner—and his conscience—from the final act. As previously noted, one blank rifle was used in the firing squad and gallows were constructed in Colorado, Connecticut, and Wyoming in which the condemned himself activated the mechanism by stepping on the trap door. Sometimes two or three "hangmen" simultaneously pulled ropes to open the trap door. And, in the case of today's lethal injection executions, frequently two people inject the drugs, only one of whom is actually injecting the lethal dose.

Our modern methods of execution have removed the executioner from any physical (intimate?) contact with the condemned. He doesn't measure him for the drop, he doesn't interview him for attitude and mental state, and for the most part he never has communication or contact with the condemned. The inmate is watched over during the death watch by one "specialty team," strapped down by another, and the body removed by yet another. Training consists of psychological techniques that instruct those involved in physical contact with the condemned in how to avoid personalizing the experience. One of these is the advice to never look the condemned man in the eye while in the process of strapping him down. This was a lesson learned early on by Robert Elliot as he began his career:

> As I made the electrode firm, I followed an irresistible impulse. I glanced up into the impassive face of the condemned man, and my eyes caught the burning, baleful glare of his. I saw fear registered there. But there was also hate—uncompromising hate for those who were doing the same thing to him that he had done to [another]. . . . It was the first time I had ever looked into the eyes of an individual on the brink of eternity. The blaze of those blue eyes held mine. I was as though hypnotized. . . . A strange sensation passed over me, I could not move. Neither could I take my eyes from his. . . . Since that morning, I have . . . never again . . . looked into the eyes of another condemned person.[88]

There are those who suggest, and I concur, that the sterility of our modern execution process is epitomized by the increasing use of lethal injection—a sterility in method and process. I have sat with the condemned as they await their executions. As a rule, they are ignored by the warden and alienated from the process and as much human contact as possible. They are fed and observed through small openings, they sit alone in their death watch cells under constant supervision with little conversation. Whereas, previously, the warden often shared the last meal with the condemned, he now eats alone or shares with a family member when permitted. And his last words, which used to be expressions of gratitude to the warden and staff, now, for the most part ignore these people. It is not always so. In one execution I witnessed, some of the corrections staff were asked to be witnesses, and even the last request for bubble gum was honored. My observations and experiences have seen both the sterility of those participating in their first execution and the familiarity bred of experience and confidence of those participating in subsequent executions. Yet, as a rule and nationwide, those who do our work for us do so at a distance.

It is, perhaps, a sign of the times that those who do such work feel it necessary to distance themselves from the experience in order to protect their own sensibilities. It is obviously done at great personal cost. Ultimately each person must develop his or her own rationale for participation in the process. Robert Elliott did so as follows:

> Each time I send a human being hurtling into eternity to face final judgement, I realize that I am partly responsible for his death. But my responsibility is no greater than that of any member of society that demanded this person's life. . . . Remember that those who administer man's justice are not acting of their own accord. They are servants of the state, nothing more; and what they do is in compliance with the mandates of the public as expressed in law. When they send a human being to his eternal doom, they do so only because it is their sworn duty. That is my philosophy.[89]

QUESTIONS FOR DISCUSSION

1. Do you believe executions should be public? Televised?
2. To what extent should victims' families be allowed to be involved in executions? Executioners? Witnesses?
3. Does such participation assume a desire for vengeance and/or revenge? Is this a legitimate motive within a criminal "justice" system?
4. Does it take a particular type of person to be an executioner?
5. Do you believe you could carry out an execution? As a member of the victim's family? As a warden? As an executioner?

THINGS TO DO OR SEE

Read Chapter 9 of John Steinbeck's *Pastures of Heaven*. What do you believe is the point of this story? How does it relate to the process of executions? Of witnessing executions?

WHAT ARE CLEMENCIES, COMMUTATIONS, AND PARDONS?

Prior to leaving office in January 2001, President Bill Clinton granted 140 pardons and commuted 36 sentences. During his eight years in office Clinton issued a total of 456 pardons. This is a power held and exercised by all presidents and most have used it—some more than others. The first pardon was issued by President George Washington in 1792 to those who led the Whiskey Rebellion. The most pardons were issued by Franklin Roosevelt during his four-year terms in office, who granted 3,687 pardons.[90]

I sat as one of three members on one of the most powerful state boards of pardon in the United States. As a member of this board, my vote could be the determining vote as to whether another human being lived or died. Not even the governor of the state could grant clemency. The last appeal would come to the three of us and, from our decision, there was no appeal. Our word was final.

I spent many quiet hours reflecting on this ultimate power and on how I might respond. There were nightmares here. I would awake in a cold sweat. The condemned supplicant was looking at me—waiting for my vote. The other two members were split—one in favor of commutation, the other opposed. It would be my vote that would make the difference. Life or Death.

I was never called on to face this decision. Although there were executions pending during this time, I left the board before any commutation hearings were

IT'S CLINTON... HE WANTS TO BE PARDONED FOR HIS PARDONS.

scheduled. I did, later, however, sit in on two of those hearings and I felt every emotion that was felt by those sitting members of the board.

The concept of clemency has a unique and interesting history. Because the institutions of men have historically been regarded as imperfect, some mechanism of grace or mercy has usually been built into the process to rectify and ameliorate institutional decisions.

The granting of clemency has fulfilled this function in the justice system. It was intended as a means to temper the politics and regional hysteria that could accompany convictions and sentences of high-profile crimes or those that seriously offend the collective consciousness, albeit a narrow and/or provincial one.

Clemency has taken two forms—pardons and commutations. Pardons represent that fact of clemency that, when invoked, entirely abrogates legal punishment. Commutation is the mitigation of criminal punishment through the substitution of a lesser sentence for a greater one.

In earlier times, clemencies were granted by the state or pontiff as a gesture of grace during holidays or special times of the year. Such clemencies became known as "holiday" or "Yuletime" clemencies. For example, before the time of Christ, the Jews had the custom of granting pardons during Passover. There were also such things as "divine intervention" clemencies that resulted when earthquakes, storms, floods, or other such natural disasters interrupted executions in process. Such occurrences were taken as signs of the deity's displeasure with the proceedings and the condemned was released. And, of course, there were the western "broken rope" clemencies that brought about the release of a person being hanged if the rope broke.

Among the Romans and later during the Middle Ages in Europe, some rather interesting pardon procedures developed. In Germany, for example, the condemned could obtain release if his wife or sweetheart ran around the prison three times in the nude. In some countries, whenever the coffers were depleted, pardons were sold as a means of raising revenue.

In this country, during the early twentieth century, pardons were also available for purchase or through political favor:

- Governor Walton of Oklahoma pardoned 603 prisoners in eleven months, some even before the judge had pronounced sentence.
- Governor Donaghey of Arkansas pardoned 361 convicts in one day.
- Texas Governor James Ferguson granted 1,774 pardons between 1915 and 1917.
- Governor W. P. Hobby granted 1,319 pardons between 1917 and 1921.
- Governor Miriam (Ma) Ferguson, also of Texas, granted 384 pardons between 1925 and 1926.

It is not possible to know which of these, if any, were purchased or the result of political patronage. The numbers, however, are certainly significant enough to raise some questions. Some governors granted pardons or commutations because of their own personal opposition to the death penalty; others acted as a last act of defiance before leaving office.

- Governor Cruce of Oklahoma opposed capital punishment and commuted twenty-two death sentences from 1911 to 1915.
- Governor Toney Anaya of New Mexico, prior to leaving office in 1986, commuted the death sentences of the five men on death row. In a prepared statement he wrote:

  As I have stated repeatedly, my personal beliefs do not allow me to permit the execution of an individual in the name of the State.[91]

To be sure that those on death row would not be executed by his successor in office, Governor Anaya chose to commute their sentences.

- Governor Richard Celeste granted commutations to eight Ohio death row inmates, including four women, because of what he believed were issues of "mental retardation or mental disorders."[92]

Among those reasons used in this country for granting pardons and commutations are the following:

- Excessive sentences
- Bargains for information on other crimes

- In exchange for testimony against others
- In exchange for assistance during prison breaks or information about planned escapes
- For help during disasters or emergencies (i.e., Governor Harriman granting commutations when inmates assisted during an airplane wreck on Rikers Island)
- In exchange for medical experiments

In addition to such reasons, some governors used a form of "Yuletime" clemency to reduce sentences or to pardon offenders during Christmas time. It was felt that such actions were particularly helpful because they held out hope for long-term inmates and helped control their behavior.

Although the intent has been to provide a mechanism for mercy within the system, clemencies have also been subject to political influences. In 1984, North Carolina's Velma Barfield became the first woman executed since the *Furman* decision. Her execution was scheduled by a Republican judge, just two days before an election in which Governor Hunt, a Democrat, was running for the Senate. In a state predominantly in favor of capital punishment, Hunt chose not to commute Barfield's sentence but still lost the election to his Republican opponent.

Governor Pat Brown of California got involved in the middle of international politics. Caryl Chessman was scheduled to be executed February 19, 1960. As the governor contemplated his decision whether to commute, he received a call from the State Department in Washington. He was informed that President Eisenhower's trip to Uruguay would be marred by "unfriendly demonstrations" if Chessman were put to death. In light of that, Governor Brown granted a sixty-day reprieve. Chessman was executed May 2, 1960.

Other governors have wrestled with the awesome power of clemency. New York's Governor Al Smith called it, "the Governor's own private Gethsemane. . . ."[93] Governor Averill Harriman felt the experience of granting pardons was particularly meaningful and a moving part of his role as governor. "[T]he exercise of clemency has brought me a deepened sense of mercy and compassion," he said.[94]

Some states vest the entire power of clemency solely in the state's governor, some give him assistance through advisory boards, and some states, like Utah, have independent boards of pardon with full authority to exercise clemency powers. Governor Harriman felt the power was best left in the hands of the governor:

> In some utopian age every punishment will fit every crime perfectly. Until then, the power of clemency will be needed to set aside the extreme penalty where the law is inflexible and to weigh factors that the judge and jury could not take into consideration.
>
> After three years as governor, I am convinced that mercy is no job for a committee. Sitting alone in his office with the ancient, awesome power of clemency, the governor must take on the most difficult tasks of all; he must become the conscience of the people of his state.[95]

It is an interesting argument that the power of clemency is vested in specifically designated people so as to provide a means of bypassing the justice system, bound as it is with rules of evidence and lawyers' manipulation, in such a way as to allow justice to be tempered by mercy. Advocates of the death penalty can perhaps feel more comfortable knowing that clemency is available to those who are unfairly sentenced to death. Opponents to the death penalty have an alternative to fighting the legal system through the clemency process. Governor Winthrop Rockefeller, who commuted the death sentences of all fifteen men on Arkansas's death row on December 29, 1970, suggested to abolitionists of the death penalty:

> This almost exclusive reliance on the courts is unfortunate. It emphasizes lawyers and legal theory when the real question is one of morals. . . . The fate of these people (on death row) can be altered by the use of a device that has been virtually ignored as a means of abolishing the death penalty—executive clemency.[96]

Perhaps, as with capital punishment in general, more time, effort, and study should be invested in the process, power, and politics of pardons and commutations. The more we know the less we will have to rely on emotion and specious arguments.

QUESTIONS FOR DISCUSSION

1. Who should be allowed to grant pardons? Governors? A board? Presidents?
2. Should there even be such a thing as a pardon?
3. For what reasons should pardons be available?
4. Should a pardon be considered a form of mercy regardless of evidence or guilt, or should it have to be based on new evidence and equally available to all as a legal right and subject to due process?
5. To what extent have pardons been political? Is the potential still there? How would you limit it?
6. Do you think the system ever makes mistakes and is that a good reason for the existence of pardons?

THINGS TO DO OR SEE

1. As a class, research and review cases in which pardons have been granted. Would you have granted a pardon in this case?
2. Can you name and identify other cases in which you would have granted a pardon? In which you would not have granted a pardon?

WHAT IS A FEDERAL EXECUTION AND HOW IS IT CONDUCTED?

I attended the Timothy McVeigh execution as a government witness. This was made possible because of my past contact with Senator Orrin Hatch of Utah and the cooperation of Attorney General John Ashcroft. Senator Hatch had been aware of my interest and research in the execution process and arranged for me to be present as an assigned staff member of the Senate Judiciary Committee, which has the oversight responsibility for the Department of Justice.

The execution of Timothy McVeigh on June 11, 2001, was the first federal execution since 1963. McVeigh was sentenced to die for bombing the Murrah Building in Oklahoma City—the worst domestic act of terrorism on U.S. territory, up to that time. This occurred on April 19, 1995, and resulted in the deaths of 168 people, including nineteen children. The execution was conducted in the first execution chamber specifically constructed by the federal government to do its own executions. Prior to this time, all federal executions took place in the states where the crime occurred, in state facilities (even in those states that had no death penalty), and under the direction of the U.S. Marshal's Office.

Witnesses

I was present as a government witness. In addition to the designated U.S. marshal and the warden, there were four specific groups allowed to witness this federal execution:

- McVeigh was allowed to have a total of six witnesses. His two attorneys were on the list as was Gore Vidal, who was scheduled to write an article for *Vanity Fair*. Vidal did not show up.
- Eight family members of victims, but for the McVeigh execution there were ten, selected by lottery.
- Ten members of the press, also chosen by lottery.
- Bureau of Prison witnesses—myself and five others.

In addition, for the first time, an execution was televised by closed circuit to Oklahoma City where the families of other victims could also witness the execution. There were 1,000 family and rescue workers in the database who were eligible to witness the execution. As it turned out, only 320 of these registered to be present. Of these, 232 showed up that morning for the "broadcast" and thirty to thirty-five of these left after the orientation, which was held to explain how the execution would proceed and what they would be seeing.

Because this was a new facility and a new procedure, there were several legal issues that arose and needed to be resolved. These included:[97]

- Whether to enforce noncontact attorney visits on the death row unit (Special Confinement Unit—SCU). The department chose not to.
- Whether attorneys could be present while McVeigh was being prepared for execution. The department denied this in order to protect the identity of the staff involved in the execution process.
- Whether there was a First Amendment right for a private company to broadcast the actual execution over the Internet. No such right existed.
- Whether the media were entitled to personal interviews, face-to-face, with condemned inmates. They had no such right.
- The extent to which the department had authority to deal with problem demonstrators on the grounds of the prison.
- Whether the actual execution could be videotaped for later use as a part of ongoing prosecution charging death by lethal injection is cruel and unusual punishment. The department prevailed by arguing that the regulations and protocol prohibited any visual photographs or recordings of an execution.

This last one was in litigation right up to the last minutes. In addition, one other suit filed by a California attorney attempted to stay the execution because he, the attorney, was attempting to have the election of George W. Bush set aside and himself declared president. Once this happened, his first official act would be to pardon McVeigh. He wanted to be sure McVeigh would still be alive to receive this pardon.

Execution Protocol

Each time I witness an execution, I am confronted with the decision of what to wear. I have never quite resolved it—nothing too formal; nothing too gaudy or frivolous; something between casual and dressy. This time I wore slacks, a shirt, and tie.

As a government witness I was taken in first. My notes reflect the procedure as I observed it:

6:49 A.M. (Central Time)

The curtain opens, Timothy McVeigh is laying on the gurney staring straight up. The IV has already been inserted into his right leg and he is covered from the neck down with a sheet. His hands are down at his side. He swallows, twitches his nose as though it itches. He closes his eyes, swallows hard, squirms, grimaces, opens his mouth, licks his lips.

Witnesses to the execution

About 30 people will witness the May 16 execution of Timothy McVeigh at the federal penitentiary in Terre Haute, Ind. Some 300 more survivors and relatives of victims of the bombing will view the execution via close-circuit television from Oklahoma City.

Officer's station

Cell

Chemical room

Execution facility

Witnesses selected by inmate.

Staff

Media

Families of victims, survivors of bombing.

Execution room
The warden will read portions of the judgment and order.

Diagram of federal execution facility at Terre Haute and procedure for McVeigh execution. Federal Bureau of Prisons. Reprinted by permission.

He looks uncomfortable. He coughs, runs his tongue around the inside of his mouth. Moves his head back and forth. He lifts his head off the gurney—looks around. He is being given a drink—the warden holds his head up so he can drink. His hair is cut close—not shaved but cut very close. He stretches his neck. [The lights now go out in the government witness room where I and five other "officials" wait.] McVeigh's eyes are closed. He is swallowing hard again, twitching his nose.

7:04 A.M.

The curtain opens for the other witnesses, the media, and victim's witnesses. I can see the media witnesses on my right, the others are on my left. McVeigh raises his head and looks around. The warden states, "Timothy McVeigh, you may make your last statement." McVeigh says nothing, just continues to stare straight up—in the direction of the camera that is aimed down at him.

7:09 A.M.

As I write these words, Timothy [not Tim] McVeigh is dying on the gurney before me. His eyes blink and then close. He coughs, puffs out his cheeks, partially opens his mouth. The green light above me comes on indicating the second drug has been administered. His eyes are partially opened and so is his mouth. He looks somewhat pale and yellowish.

7:13 A.M.

The red light comes on indicating the final drug has been administered. There is no movement or change. I look at McVeigh and then at the monitor in our room which shows the Oklahoma City feed.

7:14 A.M.

(Central Time) McVeigh is declared dead.

7:15 A.M.

The curtains are closed.

No matter how well planned and rehearsed an execution might be, there are always things that create "antacid moments" for those involved. For the McVeigh execution there were several:

- The night before the execution a man driving a pickup was arrested near the prison. He was drunk and was driving with a loaded pistol on the seat beside him. In the back of the truck they found what was thought to be bombs.
- Early on the morning of the execution, state police stopped a woman dressed in a wedding gown. She had two wedding rings and was on her way to the prison to marry Timothy McVeigh.

In addition to these two incidents, there were others more directly related to the execution itself:

Panic. At 7:01 A.M., just prior to opening the curtains for the other witnesses, they decided to test the sound and video in the death chamber for broadcast to Oklahoma City. There was none. For three minutes there was "controlled" panic until technicians resolved the problem. The curtains opened at 7:04 A.M.

Last Statement. There was great concern that McVeigh would say something in his last statement that would exacerbate the harm already done to the victims' families. There was some discussion as to whether he should even be allowed to make a statement or the extent to which it should be censored. There was relief when he made no verbal statement but, instead, had handwritten a copy of the poem "Invictus," by William Ernest Henley, which was distributed to the press.

Autopsy. There was some dispute over whether to grant McVeigh's demand that no autopsy be performed. The Bureau of Prisons (BOP) wanted one, not necessarily to show the cause of death, but rather to document that McVeigh had not been mistreated prior to his execution and to show that the drugs had been administered correctly. The county medical pathologist stated he would not pronounce McVeigh dead without an autopsy. The dispute was eventually settled—no autopsy and the cause of death would be listed as "homicide."

Removal of the Body. McVeigh's body remained in the execution facility for quite some time. The problem was that prison authorities wished to remove it quietly and without undue media coverage, but the media had posted cameras and reporters at every possible avenue of exit—including crews at the only mortuary in town that did cremations. The media had received word that McVeigh wished to be cremated and had, thus, covered that option as well. There was even a suggestion that the prison use several decoy vans in removing the body.

Media and Public Relations, Accommodations, and Prison Management. The McVeigh execution was to take place early on the morning of June 11, 2001. The night before, June 10, 2001, was to be the third game of the NBA playoffs—a game between the LA Lakers and the Philadelphia 76ers. With the execution pending, the prison had ordered a lock-down but, wisely, did allow the inmates to stay up to watch the game. Otherwise, they had anticipated some problems from the rest of the prison population. This concession seemed to ease the tension in the prison.

In addition to this realistic attitude in dealing with the inmates within the prison I also saw evidence of the value of realistic thinking in dealing with two other groups—the media and protestors.

I have observed situations in which both media and protestors are at best tolerated and at worst almost intentionally inconvenienced. In Terre Haute, however, the rational was more enlightened. In essence it was, "Rather than fight them, acknowledge that they will be there either way and have as good a relationship as possible." To this end, the warden and BOP officials met with the media and asked them what their needs were and then discussed how they could accommodate them.

They also met with the leaders of various protest groups—pro and con— and got their input about their needs as well as explaining to them what rules and restrictions the prison required—what they could and could not do. Consequently, they set up specific areas in town where each group (pro and con) could meet. Starting after midnight, and after checking them for contraband, and so on, the prison bussed them to their staging area. Each bus was preceded and followed by a police car with lights flashing. Each area was in a grassy area, lighted with floodlights, provided with portapotties and bales of straw for seating. There were also ample security personnel patrolling each area.

My Observations

Upon my arrival on June 10, the day before the execution, I found the city of Terre Haute very crowded. As it turned out, after a stay of execution from the original date of May 16, 2001, the execution had been rescheduled to take place at the same time as the sixty-first annual Miss Indiana Scholarship Program being hosted in Terre Haute. Not only were people everywhere, the media and protestors were also there. All the hotels and motels were booked and traffic was a constant problem.

That first day, I was taken to the prison and given a tour of the entire facility, as well as a detailed tour of the Special Confinement Unit (SCU) where the federal death row inmates were kept.

Early the next morning (6:00 A.M.), I was escorted to the prison. Because there was ample time before it was necessary for me to be at the staging area for government witnesses, my escort and I strolled through the protest areas. They were just beginning to gather in significant numbers. There weren't a great many at the area for those favoring the death penalty. Approximately thirty to thirty-five people sat around or held their homemade signs. Those protesting the death penalty in general and the McVeigh execution in specific were more numerous, almost 200. Most of them sat on the grass and held candles. Some of them were obviously posing themselves for the cameramen who surrounded them. Some had their heads on each others' shoulders, others were in an attitude of prayer, some were holding hands, and some were staring into the flames of their flickering candles. These people, too, had posters and placards:

"God said don't kill (even him)."

"America doesn't need closure it needs forgiveness."

"Don't kill in my name."

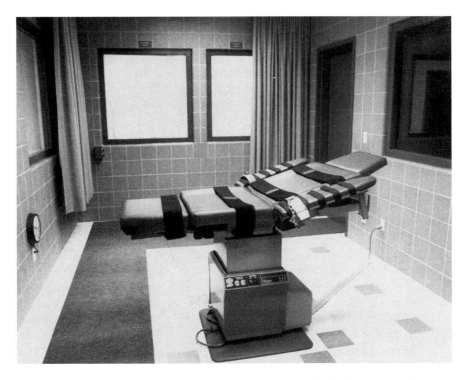

Newly constructed death chamber at Terre Haute, where Timothy McVeigh was executed.
Federal Bureau of Prisons. Reprinted by permission.

Everything was very quiet and almost surreal in the early morning mist and somber Indiana countryside.

As to the execution itself, every action was followed and reported in great detail, even McVeigh's last meal of two pints of mint chocolate chip ice cream. Within hours, however, following the execution, the men patrolling the area with M-16's, the trucks with satellite dishes, and all the roadblocks disappeared. Twenty men remained on death row awaiting their own deaths. And two weeks later there were nineteen left as Juan Raul Garza died in that same execution chamber, on that same gurney, with hardly any notice or inconvenience.

Documenting Federal Executions

Documenting, or even defining, federal executions is a frustrating experience. There must, of course, be the distinction drawn between federal and military executions as well as allowing for executions in the District of Columbia. Records and documentation are scant and scarce and, where they exist, consist mostly of numbers and statistics. Yet, behind all of these executions are actual faces and stories that are, for the most part, unknown to the public. Although my numbers vary from those gathered by others, I have tried to trace, where possible, the actual events surrounding the crimes and executions of those who died at the hands of the federal government. Since most of these occurred on Indian reservations and at a time when accurate records were not kept, this list is not complete. It does, however, highlight those that are more recent.

1790–1900. It is generally agreed that the first federal execution was that of Thomas Bird who was hanged June 25, 1790. His crime was murder and piracy. It was charged that he and a codefendant, Hans Hansen, age 19, fatally shot Captain John Conner, the master of a ship returning from Africa. According to Bird, the captain returned from shore, found the crew asleep, and beat the chief mate to death. Bird and Hansen then shot Captain Conner to death while he slept and, upon the ship's return to New England, both were arrested and tried. Hansen was acquitted whereas Bird was sentenced to death. He was hanged in Portland, Maine, before a crowd that, "was judged to be not less than three thousand or four thousand, who generally paid a decent attention to the solemn religious exercises of the day."[98] There is no record of his last words, last meal, or even where he was buried.

Since this first federal execution of Thomas Bird, figures have varied with regard to the actual number who have died. According to Watt Espy, the total number is 336 men and four women.[99] Of course, the last two federal executions of Timothy McVeigh and Juan Raul Garza would need to be added to this list.

Of the approximately 189 executions that took place during this period of 1790 to 1900, many were Native Americans who were executed for crimes committed on reservations. Additionally, there were crimes committed on the high seas and, of course, the execution of the conspirators involved in the assassination of Abraham Lincoln. These executions of the "Lincoln Conspirators" present a definitional problem. Although the crime was committed in the District of Columbia, which is under federal control, the trial was conducted by a military commission. I have chosen to define these executions as federal—even though it was not a federal offense to assassinate a president until after the assassination of President John F. Kennedy in 1963.

On July 7, 1865, 48-year-old Mary E. Surratt and three coconspirators were hanged for their role in the assassination of President Abraham Lincoln. Mrs. Surratt, George A. Atzerodt, David E. Herold, and Lewis Thornton Powell (a.k.a. Payne or Paine) were all hanged together in the old Washington Penitentiary, by hangman Christian Rath. There were numerous pleas on behalf of Mrs. Surratt because she was a woman and because her only involvement was based on the fact that her boarding house (now a Chinese Restaurant at 604 H Street) was used as a meeting place to plan the assassination. When President Andrew Johnson was asked to commute her sentence, he refused by stating, "She kept the nest where the egg was hatched."[100]

On October 18, 1895, two men, Thomas St.Clair and Hans Hansen, were hanged in the loft of San Quentin's Jute Mill. Their offense was murder on the high seas of mate Maurice Fitzgerald on the ship *Hesper.* St.Clair, the leader, and Hansen plus a third man, Sparf, planned a mutiny and, in conspiracy with other crew members, planned to seize the ship and kill the officers. They began with Fitzgerald who, as second mate, was the most unpopular on the ship. After Fitzgerald was killed, the mutiny fizzled and all three men were arrested. A 46-year-old native of Ireland, St.Clair was identified as the actual murderer and, it was claimed, had also served time in a Hong Kong prison for another murder. He was found guilty and sentenced to die. Hansen, a native of Denmark, was sentenced to die as well, but Sparf was spared because of his cooperation with authorities. A double scaffold was erected and both died together. The *San Francisco Chronicle* reported:

> The execution is unique in that it will be the first one conducted under the Federal auspices in the history of the State and the first of its kind in any State since President Johnson's Administration.[101]

1900–1929.   Although some observers note a total of eighty-three executions during this period of time, I have the personal documentation of only two.

John B. Goodwin, claiming he was not a "half-breed," was hanged in Globe, Arizona, for killing Fred Kilbe and Alfred Hillpot while they were hunting on the San Carlos Indian Reservation. The execution took place May 13, 1913. This was the first execution under federal authority to be conducted in Arizona. Actually, Arizona authorities refused to permit the execution to take place in the state prison and so he was hanged in the Gila County Jail. There is no record as to the fate of his codefendant William Stewart.

I have only limited information and documentation of one other execution that took place during this period of time. James H. Aldermon was hanged August 17, 1927, in the Broward County Jail, Fort Lauderdale, Florida.

1930–2000.   Although some statistics show sixty-seven executions during this period of time, I have been able to independently document only thirty-nine. The U.S. Bureau of Prisons counts thirty-three and others count thirty-four, excluding those executed under federal jurisdiction in the District of Columbia. I don't know why these were excluded. For a complete list, as I have documented them, see Appendix A.

On September 5, 1930, Carl Panzran was hanged at USP Leavenworth. His crime was the murder of a prison laundry foreman. His execution, within the borders of the state of Kansas, was unique because it was the first execution in Kansas since 1870. Kansas had no death penalty. It had been abolished long before Panzran's execution.

There were three executions in 1936 and eight in 1938. Most of these were for crimes of kidnapping, killings of federal agents, or killings committed during bank robberies.

In 1942, six German spies were executed in the Washington, D.C. jail. They all died within hours of each other. They were tried by a military commission appointed by President Roosevelt. They were put ashore by German submarines—four at Amagansett Beach in Long Island, New York, and four at Ponte Vedra Beach near Jacksonville, Florida. The New York crew consisted of Heinrich Harm Heinck (35), Robert Quirin (34), Ernest Peter Burger (36), and George John Dasch (39). The group that landed in Florida included Herbert Hans Haupt (22), Edward Kerling (33), Herman Neubauer (32), and Werner Thiel (35). Dasch and Burger were spared the death penalty due to their cooperation with authorities. The other six died in the electric chair.

Five executions took place in 1948, including the deaths of Samuel Richard Shockley and Miran Edgar Thompson who died in San Quentin's gas chamber December 3, 1948, for their part in the famous "Battle of Alcatraz."

Two couples comprised the four executions conducted by the federal government during 1953 and, for the first time since Mary Surratt's execution, women were executed under federal authority.

In spite of pleas from their two young sons, Ethel and Julius Rosenberg died in Sing Sing's electric chair. They were sentenced to die for espionage, that is, selling atomic bomb secrets to the communists. Harry Truman was president when the Rosenbergs appealed for clemency but he left office a few days later and it was up to newly elected President Eisenhower to make a decision. He refused their appeal stating, "by immeasurably increasing the chances of atomic war, the Rosenbergs may have condemned to death tens of millions of innocent people all over the world."[102] The Rosenbergs were executed June 19, 1953.

In an interesting side note to history, David Greenglass, brother of Ethel Rosenberg and the witness on whose testimony she was convicted, recently recanted his sworn testimony. In Sam Roberts's book *The Brother* and in a TV interview for CBS's *60 Minutes II*, Greenglass admitted, "I had no idea they would give them [the Rosenbergs] the death sentence."[103] He admitted lying about Ethel's involvement by indicating she had typed his spy notes, which were to be sent to Moscow. His wife supported his testimony, but now, he admitted, "I don't know who typed it, frankly, and to this day I can't remember that the typing took place. I had no memory of that at all, none whatsoever."[104] He claimed to have implicated Ethel in exchange for keeping his wife out of prison. When asked if he is ever haunted by the fact that he probably sent his sister to her death in the electric chair, he stated, "My wife says, 'Look, we're still alive.' "[105]

A little over six months later, Carl Austin Hall and Bonnie Brown Heady died in Missouri's gas chamber, side by side. They were prosecuted under the federal "Lindberg Law," enacted in 1932 following the kidnapping of Charles Lindberg's infant son. Enacted in 1932, it made kidnapping a federal crime if the victim had been transported across state lines and provided for FBI involvement after seven days, assuming such transportation had occurred. (The law was changed in 1956 reducing the time for FBI involvement to twenty-four hours.)

On September 28, 1953, Heady, posing as his aunt, went to the French Institute of Notre Dame de Sion, a private elementary school, and picked up 6-year-old Bobby Greenlease, Jr., son of Robert C. Greenlease, a wealthy Cadillac dealer. Heady and Hall actually killed Bobby and buried his body prior to even sending the ransom note. Both were caught; both confessed; both were sentenced to die; and both died side by side in Missouri's gas chamber.

In 1957, two brothers, George (34) and Michael (32) Krull, were executed in Georgia for the crime of rape. Their victim was not killed.

Bonnie Brown Heady and Carl Austin Hall drawn as they died in Missouri's gas chamber.
Frank Miller/*The Kansas City Star.* Reprinted by permission.

On March 15, 1963, Victor H. Feguer (28) became the last man executed during the twentieth century. His death warrant was signed by President John F. Kennedy. Feguer was sentenced to die for kidnapping and murder and hanged at the Iowa State Penitentiary, Fort Madison, Iowa. There would not be another execution for thirty-eight years.

Conclusion

Peggy Broxterman, mother of Paul Broxterman who died in the Oklahoma explosion, told me witnessing the McVeigh execution did not bring her closure. Closure was when she buried her son.

For my part, witnessing the McVeigh execution brought me neither closure nor understanding. But I was not a victim. It was not my loved one who died there. Sometimes, however, I am haunted—not as much by my last view of Timothy McVeigh, dead on the gurney with his eyes and mouth partially open and staring at the camera over his chest. I am haunted by the whys. He looked at me but probably didn't see ME. As the curtains opened, he raised his head and looked at each of the windows where the four groups of witnesses stood. There was no smile, only a fixed look, eyes locking only momentarily, as if to say, "I am here and I am not flinching." Once his head was back down, his eyes focused straight ahead as if looking straight into the camera, which provided a closed-circuit connection to the victims' families in Oklahoma City. He didn't move again. What was he thinking? What was he feeling? Why was all this necessary?

Within a week, Juan Raul Garza would die a similar death for his role in the deaths of three men—two that he ordered and the third that he committed. He was convicted under the 1988 federal "drug-kingpin" law. This law mandated death for those involved in murder associated with illegal drug dealing on a large scale.

With the execution of Timothy McVeigh, the federal execution machinery had begun to operate again. Twenty men, sitting in their small cells and awaiting their turn, now know they are no longer exempt. A new century of federal executions has begun.

QUESTIONS FOR DISCUSSION

1. Should the federal death penalty be allowed in states where no death penalty statute exists?
2. Should nonmurder convictions warrant the federal death penalty (i.e., Krull brothers, Rosenbergs, German spies)?

THINGS TO DO OR SEE

1. Read McVeigh's last words—the poem "Invictus."
2. Read and discuss the book, *American Terrorist: Timothy McVeigh & the Oklahoma City Bombings* (Lou Michel and Dan Herbeck. New York: Regan Books, 2001). Discuss his background. What factors can you see that might have influenced his actions?

CHAPTER 4

CURRENT ISSUES QUESTIONS

WHAT HAPPENS WHEN THINGS GO WRONG?

The greatest fear, and the reason for meticulous timing and rehearsals, is that something will go wrong with the execution. Not only would it be embarrassing, but it would also bring tremendous pressure and negative publicity to the prison and corrections officials. It would bring the professionalism of those who conduct executions into question and cause controversy regarding capital punishment in general.

What they do when the electric chair goes on the blink

Reprinted by permission of Leigh Rubin and Creators Syndicate, Inc.

The reality is, however, that no one is immune—ropes break, trap doors fail, electric chairs malfunction, and IVs clog or pop out. Such problems are referred to as "botched" executions. During the history of England's hangmen, a myriad of executions were "botched":

- Sometimes the condemned was decapitated because the drop was miscalculated.
- In some instances, the executioner's assistant failed to get off the trapdoor before it was sprung and he fell into the hole along with the condemned.
- In one instance the trapdoor failed to open. After several attempts, the condemned man was reprieved.

The United States also has had its share of problems.

- One executioner had left the prison after an electric chair execution and was called back to finish the job because the condemned was still breathing.
- The members of a firing squad failed to hit the target—four men missed the paper circle.
- In the days of portable electric chairs in the South, sometimes the chair shorted out, blowing fuses and disrupting power in the jail and the community.
- Once, during a gas chamber execution, the condemned got loose before the pellets had been dropped, and he ran to the windows and banged on them pleading to be let out.

Even with today's technical improvements and training, there are still occasions when the death machinery fails to operate as planned. Amnesty International has documented some of these:

April 22, 1983. John Evans. Alabama. Electrocution. After the first jolt of electricity, sparks and flames erupted from the electrode attached to Evans's leg. The electrode then burst from the strap holding it in place and caught fire. Smoke and sparks came out from under the hood. Two physicians entered the chamber and found a heartbeat. The electrode was reattached to his leg. More smoke and burning flesh. Again the doctors found a heartbeat. Ignoring the pleas of Evans's lawyer, Russ Canan, a third jolt was applied. The execution took 14 minutes and left Evans's body charred and smoldering.

September 2, 1983. Jimmy Lee Gray. Mississippi. Gas Chamber. Officials had to clear the room eight minutes after the gas was released when Gray's desperate gasps for air repulsed witnesses. His attorney, Dennis Baiske . . . criticized state officials for clearing the room when the inmate was still alive. Says David Bruck, "Jimmy Lee Gray died banging his head against a still pole in the gas chamber while reporters counted his moans."

May 24, 1989. Stephen McCoy. Texas. Lethal Injection. He had such a violent phys-ical reaction to the drugs (heaving chest, gasping, choking, etc.) that one of the wit-nesses (male) fainted, crashing into and knocking over another witness.

May 7, 1992. Justin Lee May. Texas. Lethal Injection. May had an unusually violent reaction to the lethal drugs. According to Robert Wernsman, a reporter for the *Item* (Huntsville), May "gasped, coughed and reared against his heavy leather restraints, coughing once again before his body froze." Associate Press reporter Michael Graczyk wrote, "He went into a coughing spasm, groaned and gasped, lifted his head from the death chamber Gurney and would have arched his back if he had not been belted down. After he stopped breathing, his eyes and mouth remained open."[1]

As recently as 1997, Florida continued to be criticized for its use of the electric chair:

New York City medical examiner Jonathan Arden testified that convicted murderer Pedro Medina was still alive when flames shot from his head as he was being elec-trocuted March 25 in Florida's 84-year-old electric chair. . . . State officials say the chair has been fixed and want permission to perform executions, halted since March. Arden was an expert witness for condemned Florida inmate Leo Jones, whose lawyers claim the chair is cruel and unusual punishment. . . . [2]

Contrary to earlier practices and popular belief, botched executions do not mean a reprieve for the condemned. The order for execution is phrased so as to specify "until you are dead," affirming the order of the court's sentence of death.

Western history is full of anecdotes in which a broken rope saved the con-demned from being hanged. Such "broken ropes" were considered by the super-stitious to be "acts of God" and, consequently, the condemned was usually par-doned and sent on his way.

Today, the execution proceeds until it is completed and the condemned is pronounced dead.

WHY DOES IT COST SO MUCH?

I am frequently asked, "How much can four bullets cost?" My answer, "A box of 30-30 caliber bullets, 170 grain, costs $7.90 and contains twenty shells making each cost 39.4 cents or $1.57 total cost for the four rifles (one blank)." Sometimes the question is, "How much can it cost for a syringe and a needle?" That one is easy because the cost of a lethal injection involves a few more supplies, but as I have indicated in Chapter 3, that cost is $346.51. The question has also been, "How much can it cost for 2,300 volts of electricity for two and a half minutes?" That answer is somewhere around 15 to 20 cents. And, as to the question about the cost of the gas chamber, I haven't calculated it exactly but it would include the cost of five pints of sulphuric acid, a gallon and a half of distilled water (times two—one for each mixing pot), and a pound of cyanide.

I share this information because these questions that are so frequently asked (and are actually made more like statements) are based on two faulty assumptions:

- That calculating the cost of an execution can be limited to the simple cost of bullets and syringes
- That the large number of appeals involved in death penalty cases is the reason executions cost so much

There are many conflicting statistics and numbers when it comes to assessing the cost of executions. There are also many ways of defining what is actually being priced. These definitions and calculations may vary depending on one's position on capital punishment—pro or con. I am most dangerous when claiming to be objective; however, I have tried to make my position on capital punishment clear (see Chapter 1) and, therefore, my attempt to understand the cost of executions can be filtered through whatever bias that position might represent.

The place to begin in this process is, I believe, to define what it is we are talking about. In the opening paragraph I calculated the cost of the actual method of execution. Obviously there is more to it than that. And, when people talk about the cost of execution, they are more frequently talking about the cost of capital punishment in general and not the cost of the execution itself. The overall picture is more complex and involves three general areas:

Legal

Custodial

Procedural

Legal.   Costanzo identifies some of these legal aspects as ". . . crime investigation, pretrial preparation, jury selection, guilt trial, penalty trial and appeals."[3] He also points out that these capital homicide trials are, by their very nature, more complicated and expensive than other trials. This point is exemplified by a study out of Los Angeles County reflecting the costs there.

TRIAL	DEFENSE ATTORNEY	DEFENSE INVESTIGATION	PROSECUTING ATTORNEY	PROSECUTION INVESTIGATION	COURT	JAIL
Capital	$385,998	$48,523	$771,996	$48,523	$506,408	$136,875
Regular	$160,058	$5,105	$320,116	$5,105	$82,188	$54,750

This comparison, then, shows the cost to Los Angeles County for a capital homicide trial as $1,898,323, whereas a regular trial without the possibility of the death penalty totals $627,322. Quite a significant difference.[4]

These costs are the result of the Supreme Court's constitutional protections afforded those accused of capital crimes. Some have referred to these safeguards as the "super due process model."[5] Such safeguards affect the process by causing:

- A more extensive jury selection procedure
- A fourfold increase in the number of motions filed
- A longer, dual trial process
- More investigators and expert testimony
- More lawyers specializing in death penalty litigation
- Automatic, mandatory appeals[6]

This same study puts the total cost of capital punishment to Los Angeles County at $2,087,926, while suggesting the cost to the county of life imprisonment without possibility of parole would be $1,448,935.

Custodial.   The second area of cost is that of custody and is related to the incarceration and control of death row inmates. Included here are:

- Cost of keeping the condemned on death row until execution
- Management and operation of even having a death row
- Building and maintenance of an execution chamber

It is not possible to calculate all of these costs. Breaking out the exact cost of incarcerating condemned inmates over and above that of other maximum-security inmates is extremely difficult to detail. Even the management and operation of such a place or status overlap with many other factors in the day-to-day operation of a prison. In some instances, such as construction and maintenance, these costs are absorbed and averaged out over the total number of executions conducted by a state. As an example, the federal government constructed a new execution facility at the federal prison at Terre Haute prior to the execution of Timothy McVeigh. The cost of the multimillion-dollar facility, when added to the cost of the McVeigh execution, would skew the cost tremendously, but each subsequent federal execution helps to average out the initial cost.

Custody costs have, however, become issues because of the desire to compare the cost of execution with the cost of a sentence of life in prison without possibility of parole. The problem is whose figures are to be used.

A pro–capital punishment Web site calculates a figure of $60,000 cost of care per year for death row inmates.[7] This same source suggests death row inmates average about six years' incarceration prior to their execution; thus, the cost over time would be $360,000 to be added to the calculation.

Other calculators put the cost of maintaining a condemned person on death row at only about $1,000 to $2,000 per inmate over that of other maximum-security inmates but suggest the average stay is ten years prior to execution.[8] Over all, it is most generally agreed that the cost of life in prison without hope of parole is significantly lower than that of execution—approximately one third or less of that of an execution.

Procedural.   This is the area that is generally thought of when discussing the cost of executions. As noted earlier, however, this is not the area of greatest cost. It is here that calculations would include:

- The death watch
- Overtime for staff and additional prison and corrections personnel
- Costs to local departments for added law enforcement (i.e., traffic, security, etc.)
- Food services and accommodations for witnesses and press
- Executioners and the actual drugs (bullets, syringes, chemicals, etc.)

I have sat in as a member of several execution planning committees. Each time it is ordered that costs be monitored carefully so as to assess actual execution expenditures. Sometimes separate cost codes have been established and even the appointment of one person to oversee and calculate such costs. To date, such figures have not been forthcoming. It is not for lack of intent that these figures don't exist. It is because of the myriad of contingencies and exigencies that arise and the question of how to calculate and how to track each of these costs.

There will continue to be a debate over the cost of executions. It is not hard to state that, over all, the cost of execution is high—perhaps too high. The numbers have varied from $2.3 million in Texas and $3.2 million in Florida for a "normal" execution but can go as high as $10 million as was the case when Florida executed serial killer Ted Bundy.[9] Interestingly enough, it has been calculated that the cost of appeals only represents a small fraction of these costs—somewhere between $170,000 and $219,000.[10]

If the debate on whether to keep or discard the death penalty hinges on economic factors, the answer is easy to decide. Whatever other issues are used to outweigh economic ones, however, will continue to overshadow that of cost.

THE NEXT STEP FOR AMERICAN JUSTICE

Eric Devericks, reprinted with permission. www.devtoons.com

HOW OLD WAS THE YOUNGEST PERSON EVER EXECUTED?

Much as women have traditionally been accorded a "protected" status—especially in the criminal justice system—juveniles have also been treated significantly differently. But, historically, it was not always so.

> In 1748, 10-year-old William York was hanged in England for murder.
>
> In 1800, a 10-year-old was hanged for "secreting notes" at the Post Office in Chelmsford.
>
> In 1801, 13-year-old Andrew Brenning was hanged publicly for stealing a spoon after breaking into a house.
>
> In 1808, a 7-year-old girl was publicly hanged.
>
> In 1831, a 9-year-old boy was publicly hanged for setting a house on fire.[11]
>
> In Canada, in 1803, a 13-year-old boy was hanged for stealing a cow.

Whereas England's hangmen were kept busy with children as young as 9 and 10 years of age, the youngest juveniles executed in the United States were a 12-year-old girl, executed in Connecticut, and two 12-year-old boys who were executed in Virginia.[12] However, the youngest person executed during the twentieth century was 14-year-old George Stinney. He was executed in Texas for the crime of murder.

Although juveniles have been executed in the past and were executed while juveniles, the issue today is less an issue of executing "kids" and more an issue of executing adults who were sentenced to die while juveniles and for crimes they committed as juveniles.

There is an ongoing debate as to the age at which juveniles should be tried as adults and for which crimes. Also at issue is the question as to whether they should be subject to the same penalties as adults, including the death penalty. Frustration with what the general public perceives as increasing violent juvenile crime has caused public officials to legislate mandatory transfer of juveniles to the adult court for specific crimes. Consequently, the demand for the execution of juveniles has increased. It has been documented that gangs, and even organized crime, use juveniles to do some of their killing. This is based on the knowledge that juveniles, if caught, will receive lesser sentences than adults. It is this knowledge that precipitates the movement to increase penalties for juveniles.

Although harsher sentences are understandable and although the increased penalties might assuage public fears, the reality is somewhat different. Over the years, although juveniles are increasingly being sentenced to death, these death sentences have generally been reversed. For example, in his research on juvenile death sentences imposed between 1973 and 1992, Victor Streib's data indicate 115 death sentences imposed, 79 reversed, 16 actually executed, and, at that time, 24 of those sentenced to death for crimes committed as juveniles still on death row.[13]

Streib's data continued through 1998 and included forty-nine more death sentences. All of these juveniles were still on death row. I have chosen to exclude them from the preceding count because the court system has not, most likely, had time to complete their appeals. It can be assumed, based on the previous data, that most of these will also be reversed.

Eventually, it is the courts that decide whether, and at what age, a juvenile will be executed. Two Oklahoma cases, both included in Streib's data, illustrate how the age issue controversy has been dealt with by the Supreme Court.

Wayne Thompson filed an appeal with the Supreme Court in 1987. In his appeal, *Thompson v Oklahoma*, he charged that the imposition of the death penalty against juveniles constituted cruel and unusual punishment and, further, that "Oklahoma is one of only three states that does not have a minimum age for imposing the sentence and does not specify age can be mitigating in a capital case."[14]

Thompson, age 16, was the youngest of four people who kidnapped and murdered Charles Keene in 1983. Keene was married to Wayne's sister Vickie. She claimed Keene had beaten her over a seven-year period and that she had even considered killing him herself. Keene was a bully with a long criminal record. Thompson claimed that Keene had once, unsuccessfully, tried to sexually abuse him. When Keene's body was found, he had been dead for three weeks and was discovered at the bottom of a small pond. He had been shot twice, his throat cut, and he had been sliced down the middle of his chest. A logging chain, attached to a concrete block, was wrapped around his feet. All four participants in the murder received the death penalty.

The Supreme Court, by a vote of 5–3, ruled in favor of Thompson and his sentence was reversed in 1988. At the same time, the Court let stand the execution of 16-year-olds. Subsequent decisions further clarified this ruling:

> In two 5–4 votes . . . the Supreme Court said the Constitution's ban on cruel and unusual punishment does not prohibit execution of juveniles as young as 16 or adults with the reasoning capacity of children.[15]

This decision had fatal implications for Sean Sellers, also from Oklahoma. Sellers discovered the bodies of his mother and stepfather, Vonda and Lee Bellofatto, in their Oklahoma City home, March 5, 1986. Police became suspicious at his lack of tears and, as they probed more deeply, eventually charged him with killing both parents as well as the shooting of convenience store clerk, Robert Bauers, six months earlier. As it turned out, Sellers bragged Bauers had been killed, "To see what it felt like to kill someone."

Because Sellers was 16 at the time of the crime, he was automatically tried as an adult and subsequently sentenced to die. While on death row, Sellers "gave his life to Christ" and began his own ministry to help young people avoid "Satanism," which he blamed for his crimes. He also became an artist and, with the help of psychiatrists, realized he had "multiple personality disorder" from previous episodes of abuse.

In spite of these discoveries and the help of one of the original jurors from his trial who pleaded for his life, he was executed at age 29 on February 4, 1999. The line had been drawn by the Supreme Court: 15-year-olds = No; 16-year-olds = OK.

HOW MANY INNOCENT PEOPLE HAVE BEEN EXECUTED?

Convicted of killing a police officer in Dallas, Texas, Randall Adams was given a death sentence. He spent twelve years awaiting his execution—at one time coming within three days of execution before the Supreme Court granted a stay. He was released from prison in 1989 only after a documentary, "The Thin Blue Line," brought national attention to his situation.

Since listening to him speak, just a few months after his release, I have gained a new sensitivity to the process leading up to conviction, long before the execution process begins. Adams himself stated that, in spite of his experience, he was still in favor of the death penalty, "but there is too much abuse and misuse. Be careful. You don't have the right to execute unless you can clean the system up."[16] It is this concern—that of an imperfect or even "corrupt" system—that causes the public concern about executing an innocent person.

In January 2000, Governor George Ryan of Illinois stopped all executions in that state and declared a moratorium stating:

> I can't support a system which in its administration has proven so fraught with error and come so close to the ultimate nightmare—the state's taking an innocent life."[17]

Governor Ryan took this action after reviewing what he called Illinois's "shameful" record since 1977—twelve men executed and thirteen others released from death row due to being either exonerated or to having had unfair trials.[18]

The debate continues and the questions linger. "How many innocent people have been executed?" In the face of mounting uncertainty and the increasing concern about executing innocent people, Dudly Sharp from the victims' rights organization called "Justice for All" is quoted as saying:

> We all know that these cases [death penalty] get the closest scrutiny imaginable. . . . [A]ll systems can be improved and the death penalty is certainly one of those systems. But . . . there has been no proof of an innocent person being executed in the past century.[19]

At the same time, the Supreme Court, in a 1993 ruling of a Texas death row inmate's appeal, stated that the defendant's "claim of 'actual innocence' was in itself not a constitutional claim. . . . [T]he constitution does not forbid the execution of an innocent man so long as that man had a fair trial at the time of his conviction."[20]

In their book *In Spite of Innocence*, Radelet, Bedau, and Putnam document and discuss what they believe to be "miscarriages of justice" involving death penalty cases. They claim to have documented over 400 convictions of innocent people in the United States since 1900.[21] They define these "miscarriages of justice" as more than "due process errors" but rather as those dealing only with "wrong-person convictions," which fall into two categories: (1) those in which there was no victim (e.g., victim turns out not to be really dead or, in the case of rape, it was actually consensual) and (2) those cases in which the wrong person was convicted.[22] In addition, they point to what they believe to be two dozen executions of innocent men. Among these they identify J. Adams, Anderson, Applegate, Bambrick, Becker, Cirofici, Collins, Dawson, Garner, Grzechowiak, Hauptmann, Hill, Lamble, Mays, McGee, Rybarczyk, Sacco, Sanders, Sberna, Shumway, Tucker, Vanzetti, and Wing.[23] Five of these, for me, raise some interesting issues with regard to the execution of innocent men, particularly and with regard to the death penalty in general.

The Execution of Accomplices.   Edward Applegate was executed at the same time as Mary Francis Creighton, on July 16, 1935, in New York's electric chair. As already noted, she was executed while still unconscious. (See Chapter 2.) Applegate, for the most part, was a first offender. He did admit to having sex with Creighton's 15-year-old daughter, Ruth, and wanting to marry her. Creighton felt it necessary to get rid of Applegate's 300-pound wife so this could happen. Applegate's wife was poisoned in a fashion that was similar to the poisoning of Creighton's crippled brother and that of her husband's parents. She was acquitted of these murders prior to having ever met Applegate. There was never any evidence that Applegate ever participated in the killing of his wife other than the testimony of Mrs. Creighton, although he did admit to being with her when the poison was bought.[24] Obviously he deserved punishment for his involvement. The question for me is whether he, or other accomplices who do not participate in the actual killing, deserve to be excuted.

Publicity and Notoriety.   Richard Bruno Hauptmann was tried and convicted of the kidnapping and murder of the baby son of Charles A. Lindberg in 1932. Lindbergh was a national hero and he and his wife Anne Morrow Lindbergh were the darlings of American society—young, attractive, energetic, and socially connected. The loss of their child, 20-month-old Charles A. Lindberg Jr., created tremendous public attention. Eventually Richard Hauptmann, a German immigrant, was arrested and tried under circumstances amounting to a national circus:

> For Hauptmann's trial spectators came in an avalanche, from all corners of the United States and beyond for, as H. L. Menken said, it was the greatest story since the Resurrection. . . . As a result there was hardly a paper in America that didn't send a correspondent; some sent several, and the Hearst Press sent fifty.[25]

Amidst all this furor, Hauptmann was found guilty and sentenced to die in Sing Sing's electric chair. Issues of contaminated evidence (even manufactured evidence), political intrigue, and lack of physical evidence—including the ransom money itself—still cause many to doubt the verdict and Hauptmann's actual guilt. He died in the electric chair April 3, 1936.

Throughout her life, Hauptmann's wife, Anna, who said Hauptmann was with her the entire evening of the kidnapping, maintained his innocence. She petitioned presidents and governors for a posthumous pardon for her husband. Hauptmann was even retried in a mock trial held in Flemington, New Jersey, site of the original trial. This time he was found not guilty. Still, no pardon—no one would give her any hope or consideration. She died in 1994, maintaining his innocence and stating, in a 1988 interview:

> The pity I feel for the people who do this thing. Ach, they stoop so low. How must they feel thinking, ach, I was the one who sent that man to his death. Because they know. They all have to die, and with all their money and with all their titles they will go the same way, and when their hour comes they will be afraid. I am not afraid.[26]

Immigrants and Posthumous Pardons.   On August 23, 1927, Nicola Sacco and Bartolomeo Vanzetti were executed. And, in 1977, on the fiftieth anniversary of their executions, they were pardoned by Massachusetts Governor Michael Dukakis. These two Italian immigrants were active as "anarchists" and participated in strikes, picketing, and passing out handbills. They were active in ongoing demonstrations against capitalism and its intendant evils. Sacco, a shoemaker, and Vanzetti, a "fish peddler," were arrested, tried, and sentenced to die in Massachusetts for their participation in two crimes—a payroll holdup in Bridgewater (unsuccessful) and a double murder in Braintree, also involving a payroll. They were tried amid fears of the "red scare" and they were used by other radical groups, including communists, socialists, and anarchists who were grouped together as part of a Sacco-Vanzetti Defense Committee.[27] To the detriment of Sacco and Vanzetti these groups used the case and its high profile to serve their own ends.

The case is complicated and includes several other "characters" who probably had more culpability in the crimes than did Sacco and Vanzetti. Circumstantial evidence, a failure to understand the American criminal justice system, and, to some extent, suspected collusion and deceit on the part of friends and even attorneys all had a part in the final outcome. There is also a hint of martyrdom in a last interview with Vanzetti:

> If it had not been for these thing, I might have live out my life talking at street corners to scorning men. I might have die, unmarked, unknown, a failure. Now we are not a failure. This is our career and our triumph. Never in our full life could we hope to do such work for tolerance, for joostice, for man's understanding of man as now we do by accident. Our words—our lives—our pains—nothing! The taking of our lives—lives of a good shoemaker and a fish-peddler—all! That last moment belongs to us—that agony is our triumph.[28]

It is generally conceded that it was the political views of Sacco and Vanzetti along with their status as "foreigners" that tainted their trial and resulted in their death penalty and executions.

On July 19, 1977, Governor Dukakis issued a proclamation declaring August 23, 1977 (the fiftieth anniversary of their execution) as "Nicola Sacco and Bartolomeo Vanzetti Memorial Day." In doing so he acknowledged that:

- The atmosphere of their trial and appeals was permeated by prejudice against foreigners and hostility toward unorthodox political views;
- The conduct of many of the officials involved in the case shed serious doubt on their willingness and ability to conduct the prosecution and trial of Sacco and Vanzetti fairly and impartially.[29]

He then proceeded to declare:

that any stigma and disgrace should be forever removed from the names of Nicola Sacco and Bartolomeo Vanzetti, from the names of their families and descendants, and so, from the name of the Commonwealth of Massachusetts; and I hereby call upon all the people of Massachusetts to pause in their daily endeavors to reflect upon these tragic events, and draw from their historic lessons the resolve to prevent the forces of intolerance, fear, and hatred from ever again uniting to overcome the rationality, wisdom, and fairness to which our legal system aspires.[30]

Such a statement neither necessarily grants the admission of innocence that many believe Sacco and Vanzetti deserve nor does it bring them back to life. Such proclamations and/or posthumous pardons are sometimes confusing and most often too late to do any good to those whose lives have been taken. Perhaps they are granted for the peace of mind of the families and descendants. Posthumous pardons have been granted in many famous cases (e.g., Dr. Mudd who gave medical assistance to John Wilkes Booth following the assassination of President Lincoln) and in some not-so-famous cases, such as those in Idaho and Nevada wherein members of the Industrial Workers of the World (IWW or "Wobblies") have been granted posthumous pardons for crimes for which they were executed.

Speaking of posthumous pardons, one of the cases that has been debated for years is that of the execution of Joe Hill. Many, including Radelet and colleagues, believe Joe Hill was another of those who was executed because of his political leanings and activism. I became involved in this case only tangentially and, I might add, without affecting the outcome, although, had the timing been right, Joe Hill would have received a posthumous pardon.

Joe Hill (a.k.a. Joel Haegglund, Joe Hillstrom) was an itinerant worker who came to America from Sweden. He was a member of the IWW (Industrial Workers of the World), an organization that opposed the deplorable working conditions of the laborers created by capitalist interests and the labor "bosses." In support of attempts to organize the laborers, Hill composed songs and participated in rallies and demonstrations. He became quite popular in the IWW and his songs gave inspiration to the movement.

In 1914, he was in Utah when a grocery store owner was robbed and killed. The owner's son was also killed but not before he got off a shot and hit one of the two robbers. The next day Joe Hill went to a doctor to be treated for a gunshot wound. The doctor notified the police who interviewed Hill. He claimed to have received the wound as a result of a fight over a woman. When asked to give her name he refused, stating he would not ruin the reputation of a woman.

Amid the intrigue of politics, unionism, and, some charged, religious interference, Hill was found guilty and executed November 19, 1915. Among those who pleaded for his life were Helen Keller, President Woodrow Wilson, and the ambassador from Sweden—all to no avail. Radelet and colleagues state:

> Hill appears to have been an innocent victim of "politics, finance and organized religion . . . a powerful trinity"; his conviction and death are "one of the worst travesties of justice in American labor history."[31]

As I have already mentioned, I served as a member of the Utah State Board of Pardons, the only authority in the state empowered to grant clemencies, including pardons and posthumous pardons. For several years prior to my appointment, a man by the name of Folke G. Andersen, a native of Sweden, then living in California, had petitioned presidents, congressmen, the governors of Utah, the legislature, and the Board of Pardons for a posthumous pardon for Joe Hill. In one of his letters he pleaded:

> How can we human beings help that we often feel akin to his [Joe Hill] kind of an underdog or martyr when we long have sensed and found his *innocence* in a crime-infested tumult and turbulence? It truly calls for a rectification at long last from the highest of authorities. Joel Haegglund—Joe Hill—was born 100 years ago (Oct. 7, 1879), and it would seem more than appropriate [sic] to have the Utah State Board of Pardons afford and bestow a grant, finally, to relieve the burden of a once stoic and impassive, unproven judicial charge, still without proof of crime, and to declare an acquittal and exculpation for Joe Hill.[32]

Such an appeal never came to the board during my brief time as a member of that body. However, we did discuss the issue and, as far as I could tell, Joe Hill would have received a posthumous pardon had we received the petition at that time. In later conversations with Mr. Anderson, he told me he had been ill during that period of time and was unable to file such a request. I, personally, am convinced that Joe Hill was "probably" not guilty of the crime for which he was executed and, even if he was, that he did not deserve the imposition of the death penalty.

Although posthumous pardons may grant some relief to those falsely sentenced to die or already executed, there is another growing population of those who lived on death row, sometimes facing imminent execution, and who were released. Some of these releases were because they were, in fact, found to be not guilty of the crime for which they were sentenced or because they were granted a new trial and the prosecution decided not to pursue the matter. Such was the case of Florida's Juan Melendez.

In January 2002, Melendez was released from Florida's death row and given a new suit and $100. He had spent almost eighteen years awaiting his execution for murder. He argued it was another man who had done the killing and that he was not even present at the time of the killing. With the discovery of new evidence and after eighteen years, Judge Barbara Fleischer threw out the conviction and rather than retry the case, the prosecutor decided not to go back to court and Melendez was released.

The Death Penalty Information Center (DPIC) lists twenty-two other such cases in Florida and over 100 nationwide since 1973. Identifying these as "Released from Death Row, Probable or Possible Innocence," the DPIC presents some of the following specific examples:

Sonia Jacobs   Conviction 1976
Florida   Released 1992

Jacobs and her companion, Jesse Tafero, were sentenced to death for the murder of two policemen at a highway rest stop in 1976. A third codefendant received a life sentence after pleading guilty and testifying against Jacobs and Tafero. The jury recommended a life sentence for Jacobs, but the judge overruled the jury and imposed death. A childhood friend and filmmaker, Micki Dickoff, then became interested in her case. Jacobs's conviction was overturned on a federal writ of habeas corpus in 1992. Following the discovery that the chief prosecution witness had given contradictory statements, the prosecutor accepted a plea in which Jacobs did not admit guilt, and she was immediately released. Jesse Tafero, whose conviction was based on much of the same highly questionable evidence, had been executed in 1990 before the evidence of innocence had been uncovered.[33]

Lee Perry Farmer   Conviction 1992
California   Released 1999

Farmer was acquitted at a retrial in California for capital murder. He had spent nine years on death row. He was, however, convicted of burglary and being an accessory to murder. He was credited with time already served and will be released. A federal court overturned his first conviction because of incompetent counsel. Another man confessed to the murder. (*Sacramento Bee*, 1/18/99)[34]

Donald Paradis   Conviction 1981
Idaho   Released 2001

After spending fourteen years on death row, Donald Paradis was released from prison when his 1981 murder conviction was overturned. Judge Gary Haman, who originally sentenced Paradis to death, came out of retirement to accept Paradis's plea to moving the body after murder. Paradis, who always maintained that he was not involved in the slaying of Kimberly Anne Palmer, was sentenced to five years and released for time already served.

The deal came after a federal court of appeals ruled that Paradis was denied a fair trial because prosecutors withheld potentially exculpatory evidence. Paradis was scheduled for execution three times before his sentence was commuted to life imprisonment in 1996 by then Governor Phil Blatt who had doubts about Paradis's guilt.

Paradis's trial lawyer, William Brown, never studied criminal law, never tried a felony case, and never tried a case before a jury. While representing Paradis, Brown also worked as a police officer. His defense lasted only three hours. In addition, Dr. Brady, the pathologist who performed the autopsy of Palmer, testified that Palmer had been killed in Idaho, not in Washington where Paradis had already been acquitted of murder. Dr. Brady was fired as a medical examiner soon after the Paradis trial when it was discovered that he had sold human tissue for profit and saved human blood, collected during autopsies, for use in his garden. (Associated Press, 4/11/01, and *New York Times*, 4/12/01)[35]

These are only a few of the cases cited by the DPIC as evidence of possible or probable cases in which the potential for executions of innocents has been a reality. Another interesting case is that of Anthony Porter who was freed from death row in Illinois after almost sixteen years there. Sentenced to die for killing a young couple in a Chicago park, Porter steadfastly maintained his innocence. By the age of 26, he was certainly no saint and his criminal record made him the ideal suspect. An eyewitness testified against him and his conviction was a done deal—until four students in a Northwestern University journalism class took on a project. With their research and follow-up, they were able to locate the eyewitness, get him to recant his testimony, then locate the actual murderer and videotape his actual confession. Porter was released from death row and the real murderer was charged with the murder. One of the students stated:

> I don't think the police cared whether Porter did it or not. . . . I think they thought of it as some sort of preventative punishment and if he didn't do this crime, he was guilty of something.[36]

The release of men from death row happens frequently enough that there is a national conference on "Wrongful Convictions and the Death Penalty" as well as an organization for death row survivors. Some are suing the states in which they were convicted, sentenced, and incarcerated:

> Two men imprisoned for 14 years after being falsely convicted of murder filed a $60 million lawsuit against the state of New York. Anthony Faison, 35, and Charles Shepherd, 38, left prison in May after another man was arrested in the death of a taxi driver.[37]

It would appear the cost of mistakes in our justice system regarding imposition of the death penalty and the possibility of executing innocent people is continuing to increase, and could become a major factor in considering whether to continue to have capital punishment. After commuting the death sentence of a convicted killer, Governor Buddy Roemer said:

> In an execution in this country, the test ought not to be reasonable doubt. The test ought to be is there any doubt.[38]

CHAPTER 5

CONCLUSION:
WHAT HAVE I LEARNED?

For me, this question has been the most important. It is not only about the past—what I have learned—but about the present and the future—what I am learning.

After six executions, numerous hours on death row, years of studying, reading, lecturing, and teaching about capital punishment, what have I learned?

That the process is long and complicated. It is no easy thing to take a human life in the name of the state. Careful planning, intense coordination of agencies and personnel, exact attention to details and legal rights, and sensitivity to emotions, attitudes, and psyches of everyone involved all become a part of an execution. It is, for all involved, an awesome responsibility.

That those we sentence to die are not always monsters. One of the matrons present at the execution of Ohio's Anna Marie Hahn stated, just prior to the execution, "I do feel that in spite of her vanity, her conceit, her stubbornness, her guilt, some of the good things should be remembered about her—she was so human, so human."[1] This has been my experience. Not in all cases, but in those in which I have been personally involved, for the most part, these men have been " . . . so human." Their crimes have been violent and inexcusable. Their punishment extreme. Yet in each of them I have sensed their humanity. Another of the women executed during the twentieth century phrased it well. Martha Jule Beck (The Obese Ogress, Three-Hundred-Pound Lovey Dovey) was executed in New York, along with her lover, for kidnapping and murder. When the priest asked her if she had repented of her sins, she said, "I know my sin was great, but the penalty is great too. That makes things even, I guess."[2]

That those involved in the execution process are caring, compassionate human beings. I have not only been with those facing execution but also with those involved in taking the life of those who are to be executed. They face this task with courage and resolve. Whether they openly admit and discuss the impact, it is a significant event in their lives. Some show no outward emotions, others return home and weep. Some must seek counseling, others counsel with each other. Some do not return to their occupation, others return with a new sense of the value of human life and a new perspective of those they work with on the prison blocks. No matter what they do or how they cope, they feel the immense weight of taking part in society's ritual of capital punishment. Although our hand might be *symbolically* on the rope, it is their hand that is *literally* there.

Most of all, however, I have *felt* what capital punishment is. I have an understanding (*Verständnis*) of capital punishment and the execution process from a personal and emotional perspective. In addition to what I have written about my presence at Tyburn:

> I have stood at the execution gate in Russia just outside St. Petersburg's Peter and Paul fortress where hundreds of men went to their deaths. Doestoevsky was kept here and experienced the terror of being stood up to be executed by firing squad, then released.

> I have placed flowers at gallows hill just outside the Tower of London and inside the tower complex where royalty and political prisoners were executed.

> I have leaned against the execution wall inside Auschwitz and visited Dachau, where mass executions were carried out under the guise of creating a "master race."

> I have visited the guillotine in Prague. An instrument of death for those sentenced to die by the "star chamber," which sat in judgment of Czech patriots. It had been dumped in the Moldau River as the Nazis left and the Allies rescued Prague. Recovered from its watery repository, it now stands as a monument to the abuse of power.

> I have visited Australia's Goat Island in Sydney Harbor where England's transported criminals were banished and hanged. Here they suffered beatings and were often chained to the rocks to keep them from escaping.

> I have stood on the steps at the Alhondiga de Granaditas in Guanajuato, Mexico, where the severed heads of four "insurgents"—now proclaimed heroes of independence—had hung in wire baskets from hooks on the four corners of the building. Executed as traitors, their heads hung for ten years until independence for Mexico was finally won.

I have learned most seriously and most intensely that the penalty of death has awesome power—power to eliminate enemies; power to enforce ideology; power to destroy opposition; power to control; power to purge; power to sanction. I know I can't be trusted with such power—this, too, I have learned about myself. I am watchful of all those who have such power. I have learned the potential for abuse is great and the consequences of such abuse are irreversible.

Still, I stand in the middle. The death penalty is an option—one of many. However, it is one to be used with sensitivity, caution, and compassion. To do so without emotion is to imitate those we execute. To do so with compassion is to share our humanity. To do so at all is to assume deity.

ROSTER OF FEDERAL EXECUTIONS

Federal Executions

NAME/PLACE OF EXECUTION	METHOD	RACE	OFFENSE	AGE	EXECUTION DATE
Bird, Thomas Portland, ME	Hanging	White	Murder and Piracy	U	June 25, 1790
Surratt, Mary F. Old Penitentiary Washington, DC	Hanging	White	Assassination of President Lincoln	48	July 7, 1865
Atzeroot, George A. Old Penitentiary Washington, DC	Hanging	White	Assassination of President Lincoln	33	July 7, 1865
Harold, David E. Old Penitentiary Washington, DC	Hanging	White	Assassination of President Lincoln	23	July 7, 1865
Powell, Lewis Thomlon Old Penitentiary Washington, DC	Hanging	White	Assassination of President Lincoln	20	July 7, 1865
St. Clair, Thomas Loft of San Quentin's Jute Mill	Hanging	Unknown	Murder	46	October 18, 1895
Hansen, Hans Loft of San Quentin's Jute Mill	Hanging	Unknown	Murder	U	October 18, 1895
John B. Goodwin Globe, AZ	Hanging	Half Indian	Murder	U	May 13, 1913

(continued)

Federal Executions *(continued)*

NAME/PLACE OF EXECUTION	METHOD	RACE	OFFENSE	AGE	EXECUTION DATE
Aldermon, James H. Broward Co. Jail Fort Lauderdale, FL	Hanging	Unknown	Murder	U	August 17, 1927
Panzran, Carl USP Leavenworth, KS	Hanging	White	Murder	36	September 5, 1930
Barrett, George Marion Co. Jail, IN	Hanging	White	Murder	55	March 24, 1936
Gooch, Arthur Oklahoma State Prison McAlester, OK	Hanging	White	Kidnapping	27	June 19, 1936
Gardner, Earl Gila Co. Jail, AZ	Hanging	Indian	Murder	30	July 13, 1936
Booth, Arnette A. State Penitentiary, Moundsville Charleston, WV	Hanging	Unknown	Kidnapping	46	March 19, 1938
Travis, John State Penitentiary, Moundsville Charleston, WV	Hanging	Unknown	Kidnapping	25	March 19, 1938
Adkins, Orville State Penitentiary, Moundsville Charleston, WV	Hanging	Unknown	Kidnapping	25	March 19, 1938
Chebatoris, Anthony Federal Detention, Farer Milan FCI, MI	Hanging	White	Murder	39	July 8, 1938
Seadlund, Henry John (a.k.a. Peter Anders) Cook Co. Jail Chicago, IL	Electric Chair	White	Kidnapping and Murder	27	July 14, 1938

NAME/PLACE OF EXECUTION	METHOD	RACE	OFFENSE	AGE	EXECUTION DATE
Suhay, Robert J. USP Leavenworth, KS	Hanging	White	Murder	25	August 12, 1938
Applegate, Glenn J. Michigan City State Prison, IN	Hanging	White	Murder	34	August 12, 1938
Dalhover, James Michigan City State Prison, IN	Electric Chair	White	Murder	32	November 18, 1938
Nelson, Charles Federal Jail Juneau, AK	Hanging	Indian	Murder	37	November 10, 1939
Haupt, Herbert Hans Jail, Washington, D.C.	Electric Chair	White	Sabotage	22	August 8, 1942
Heinck, Heinrich Harm Jail, Washington D.C.	Electric Chair	White	Sabotage	34	August 8, 1942
Edward, John Jail, Washington, D.C.	Electric Chair	White	Sabotage	33	August 8, 1942
Neubauer, Herman Jail, Washington, D.C.	Electric Chair	White	Sabotage	32	August 8, 1942
Quirin, Richard Jail, Washington, D.C.	Electric Chair	White	Sabotage	34	August 8, 1942
Theil, Werner Jail, Washington, D.C.	Electric Chair	White	Sabotage	35	August 8, 1942
Arwood, Clyde Tennessee State Prison	Electric Chair	White	Murder	24	August 14, 1943
Ruhl, Henry Wyoming State Prison Rawlong, WY	Gas Chamber	White	Murder	36	April 27, 1945

(continued)

Federal Executions *(continued)*

NAME/PLACE OF EXECUTION	METHOD	RACE	OFFENSE	AGE	EXECUTION DATE
Nelson, Austin A. Federal Jail Juneau, AK	Hanging	Black	Murder	28	March 1, 1948
Watson, David J. Florida State Prison Raiford, FL	Electric Chair	Black	Murder	23	September 15, 1948
Shockley, Samual Richard California State Prison San Quentin, CA	Gas Chamber	White	Murder	38	December 3, 1948
Thompson, Miran Edgar California State Prison San Quentin, CA	Gas Chamber	White	Murder	31	December 3, 1948
Ochoa, Carlos Romero California State Prison San Quentin, CA	Gas Chamber	Hispanic	Murder	29	December 10, 1948
La Moore, Eugene Federal Jail Juneau, AK	Hanging	Black	Murder	U	April 14, 1950
Rosenberg, Ethel Sing Sing Ossining, NY	Electric Chair	White	Sabotage	37	June 19, 1953
Rosenberg, Julius Sing Sing Ossining, NY	Electric Chair	White	Sabotage	34	June 19, 1953
Hall, Carl Austin Missouri State Penitentiary Jefferson City, MO	Gas Chamber	White	Kidnapping and Murder	34	December 18, 1953
Heady, Bonnie Brown Missouri State Penitentiary Jefferson City, MO	Gas Chamber	White	Kidnapping and Murder	41	December 18, 1953
Puff, Gerherd A. Sing Sing Ossining, NY	Electric Chair	White	Murder	39	August 12, 1953

NAME/PLACE OF EXECUTION	METHOD	RACE	OFFENSE	AGE	EXECUTION DATE
Brown, Arthur Ross Missouri State Penitentiary Jefferson City, MO	Electric Chair	White	Kidnapping	30	February 24, 1956
Krull, George Georgia State Prison Reidsville, GA	Electric Chair	White	Rape	34	August 21, 1957
Krull, Michael Georgia State Prison Reidsville, GA	Electric Chair	White	Rape	32	August 21, 1957
Feguer, Victor H. Iowa State Penitentiary Fort Madison, IA	Hanging	White	Kidnapping and Murder	28	March 14, 1963
McVeigh, Timothy J. USP, Terre Haute, IN	Lethal Injection	White	Bombing of Federal Building	33	June 11, 2001
Garza, Juan Raul USP, Terre Haute, IN	Lethal Injection	Hispanic	Murder	42	June 18, 2001

QUESTIONS TO AND ANSWERS FROM A DEATH ROW INMATE

1. **Do you think you will ever actually be executed? Why or why not?**

I do not beleave I will ever be executed becouse I have never murdered anyone. A commonplaced stereotyped responce to my answer would be, "Thats what they all say," but the hard facts are, some of us are telling the trueth. If my constitutional rights to a fare and impartial trial would not have been violated, that fact would have been proven. It is my hopes that the higher courts will see this and give me a retrial.

2. **Other than the death penalty, what would have been a better way for the court to deal with you? What kind of sentence would you propose for those convicted of major crimes such as homicide?**

The first half of this question postulates guilt. So therefore I will not respond to it. But in responce to the second half, I have found throue experience that just becouse a person is convicted of a crime does not necessarily mean that person is guilty. But in case's where a person is convicted of a crime such as homocide, that person should be taken out of society for the protection of society if the homocide is a proven to be premeditated or for pecuniary gain or vengeance. I would not recommend this action for persons who have no other alternative but to use deadly force to protect thenself, or unknowingly or accidently couse the death of another person. I could never recommend the death of another person. I could never recommend the death penalty for anyone for a number of reason.

They are, a person can only be convicted of a crime by human beings and human beings do make mistakes. Therefore innocent people may be executed. I beleave that has happened in the past and can happen agen. To protect society from persons convicted of crimenal homocide, murder in the first degree, those person's can effectively be taken out of society and placed in a prison for as long as society wants them to be there. It is agenst the law for an individual to use deadly force to protect him or her self when it is unnecessary, so why shouldn't it be agenst the law for society or the protectors of society (The Legal Justice System) to use deadly force to protect itself or society when it is unnecessary. If this rule is not applied then we end up with a society supporting a hypacriticaLegal Justice System. There are meny arguments agenst the death penalty, but the major argument for the death penalty is that it is a deterrent. It is my belief that if a person plans to murder someone, that person will not worry about the death penalty becouse, in the first place, they believe that they are going to get away with it. It is that plain and simple. The criminal mind is not as complex as prosecutor's try to make them out to be. They like to make there job look difficult. Removing people from society is the best deterrent that I can think of at this time. I have found throue conversation with other inmates that the death penalty has a more encouraging effect then deterring on potential murderers. All of the inmates that I talk to rationalize that if they state can do it, why can't they. They see the two as legal murder and illegal murder with only an insignificant technical differance.

3. **When you were a younger person, did you ever think about the death penalty in relation to yourself?**

   No. I never ever thought about the death penalty at all. I may have saw an execution on T. V., such as in westerns, but after the program it was forgotten.

4. **If you could do things over again, would you change your past life in any way (other than not getting caught)? How?**

   I am offended about the other then not getting caught part. Other then that it is a good question.

   Yes, there are some things that I would change in my life. First and for most is, I would never have come to Utah. Second, I wish that I had never got involved in drugs the way I did. And third, I wish that I would have finished school. These are the changes I would make in my past if I could.

5. **What are your feelings about our present justice system (the police, the courts, corrections, etc.)?**

   The Legal Justice System as it is at present is not good at all. The principales and theory that are Legal Justice System is based is superlative to say the less. But the people implementing it have deranged it. Take the police for example. They have been known to take bribes on occasion. They have been know to abuse there power in every way possable. And once they get you in jail they steal from you. Most people who have not done time don't know this and don't beleave it but that don't mean it doesn't happen. And it sometimes seem to us that no one care's.

   The courts would be perfect if they only did what they say they do. It is a fact that when it comes to justice, you only get what you pay for. The more you can pay, the more justice you get, the less you pay, the less justice you get. Also the color of your skin plays a very important role in how mush justice you get. It is my belief that out of all of the factors effecting the amount of justice you get, the nature of the crime plays the less important role.

The corrections part of the Legal Justice System is a bad joke. There is no such thing as rehabilitation in prison. Prisons are being used for ponishment. The Board of Pardons has used rehabilitation as an excuse to hold some people in prison and let others go sooner then some.

The crimenal mind look at these abuses and ask, if they rich ad the people enforceing the law do not have to obey the law, why should I.

6. **Does the waiting and the lengthy appeal process bother you, or do you see it as being to your advantage? Some people have said that the appeal process itself constitutes "cruel and unusual" punishment. Would you agree?**

The appeal process it's self does not constitutes crule and unusual punishment. The lenghty appeal process can work ether for or agenst a particular defendent. Each case will have to be determine independently on it's own merits as to wheather it works for are agenst a defendent. As to whether the waiting bother me or not, a lot of things bother me, but there are some things that we learn to live with. Being in prison bothers me, not waiting court decision.

7. **If you had your choice between being executed and spending the rest of your life in prison without hope of parole, what would be your choice? Why?**

I would chouse life without parole. Because, to me there is no such thing as with out hope of parole. To me, hope is something like faith. What you hope for or have faith in, others may not be able to see or understand. If I were given life with out parole, which to some people would be a hopeless situation, I could always hope that someday, maybe 30 years from now, the law that put me here mite be changed, or I mite be able to find some kind of pursuit that would make my life meaningfull to me right here in prison.

8. **How do you feel right now? What is it like to live on death row status?**

To me it is like being in a maximum security jail. We have less privileges then the other prison inmates but that is understandable in most cases. It all depends on who is running the jail at the time. We are more comfortable now with this administration then the last one because the last one treated us like something less then vicious criminals.

9. **What is your belief about what happens to a person after death?**

I believe that we all will just sleep untill we are all resurrected by God to be judged.

10. **What should we as a class know and understand about the death penalty—from your point of view?**

You should know that the death penalty is not a deterrent of murder. It is for vengeance only. Plus, the death penalty has been used as a method of commiting suicide by suicidal people. I am not suicidal, I love life and wish to live. As long as possible.

COMMENTS

First of all I would like to thank you for being interrested in my point. The only other people interrested in my point of view was the press but only if it was something sensational. I want people to know and understand my point of view so therefore I don't have any objections to anyone other then your class examining this paper.

I was affended by questions number two and fore because they postulated or presumed us guilty. I maintain that I am not guilty of murder. But my answers to the question were not intended to deal with guilt or innocents.

I understand that different people will have different opinions about the answers that I gave to each question, all I ask is that I not be miss quoted and that my entire answer be given to any particular question. Not just half of it. I hope that the answers are helpfull and complete enough for you.

NOTES

■ ■ ■ ■ ■

CHAPTER 1   PERSONAL QUESTIONS

1. Death row interview, February 17, 1988.
2. Richard Moran, "Invitation to an Execution—Death by Needle Isn't Easy," *Los Angeles Times*, March 24, 1985, p. 6.
3. Ibid.
4. Jack Levin and James Alan Fox, *Essays in Murder and Mayhem*. Boston: Allyn & Bacon, 2001, p. 127.
5. Comment by Elliot King prior to watching the execution of the man who killed his niece. *The Salt Lake Tribune*, January 26, 1996, p. A6.
6. Associated Press, *Standard-Examiner*, "Killer Executed as Victim's Family Watches."
7. *Ogden Standard-Examiner*, April 17, 1986, p. 8A.
8. Ibid.
9. Ibid.
10. Ibid.
11. Robert Elliott with Albert Beatty, *Agent of Death: The Memoirs of an Executioner*. New York: E. P. Dutton & Co., 1940, p. 230.
12. "Execution Witnesses Complain of Access," *San Francisco Examiner*, February 23, 1996, p. A-19.
13. Ibid.
14. Elliott, p. 230.
15. Justin Atholl, *Shadow of the Gallows*. London: John Long Limited, 1954, p. 186.
16. "Executions," *Editor and Publisher*, April 22, 1989, p. 21.
17. Ibid., p. 39.
18. Ibid., p. 94.
19. Ibid., p. 39.
20. *Tribune-Star*, June 11, 2001, p. 2.
21. *Ogden Standard-Examiner*, June 12, 2001, p. 4A.
22. James W. Waters, "I Walked the Last Mile with a Condemned Man to the Electric Chair." 1958, p. 11. Unpublished copy in the author's possession.
23. "Coroner Agrees to Study Body of Spenkelink," *Ogden Standard-Examiner*, March 3, 1981.

24. Ibid.

25. Sandra Gonzales, *Knight-Rider Newspapers*, Story #17502, May 10, 1993.

26. Karl Menninger, *The Crime of Punishment*. New York: The Viking Press, 1968, pp. 198–199.

27. *Ogden Standard-Examiner,* January 16, 1985.

28. Jack Fisher, "Death Penalty Riddle Lingers: Does It Deter Killers?" *Knight-Rider Newspapers,* Story #22340, March 27, 1992.

CHAPTER 2 GENERAL QUESTIONS

1. John Timbs, *Curiosities of London*. London: David Bogue, 1855, p. 38.

2. Ibid., p. 24.

3. Justin Atholl, *The Reluctant Hangman: The Story of James Berry, Executioner 1884–1892*. London: John Long Limited, 1956.

4. Egyptian state executioner Helmi Sultan. *Newsweek*, September 9, 1991, p. 17.

5. Brian Bailey, *Hangmen of England: A History of Execution from Jack Ketch to Albert Pierrepoint*. London: W. H. Allen & Co., 1989, p. 5.

6. Samuel Midgley, *Hallifax, And Its Gibbet-Law Placed in a True Light*. Reprinted by J. Horsfall Turner, Idel, Bradford, 1886, p. 59.

7. L. Kay Gillespie, *The Unforgiven: Utah's Executed Men*. Salt Lake City, UT: Signature Books, 1997, pp. 181–182.

8. Robert G. Smith, "Hanged for Murder—A 5-Ton Elephant," *National Enquirer,* July 24, 1979; Also see the book The Day They Hung the Elephant by Charles Edwin Price, 1992. Johnson City Tennessee: The Overmountain Press.

9. E. P. Evans, *The Criminal Prosecution and Capital Punishment of Animals*. London: William Heinemann, 1906, p. 172.

10. Ibid., p. 173.

11. Ibid., p. 137.

12. Ibid., pp. 160–161.

13. Ibid.

14. Ibid., p. 189.

15. Ibid., p. 175.

16. Ibid.

17. Ibid., p. 150.

18. R. Chambers, ed., *The Book of Days: A Miscellany of Popular Antiquities*. Detroit: Gale Research Company, 1967, pp. 128–129.

19. Graeme Newman, *The Punishment Response*. Philadelphia: J. B. Lippincott Co., 1978, p. 90.

20. Psalm 51.

21. Hugo Bedau, *The Death Penalty in America: An Anthology*. Garden City, NY: Doubleday & Co., 1967, pp. 3–4.

22. Evans, p. 10.

23. Ibid., p. 16.

24. Ibid., p. 194.

25. These stories are all told in more detail in my book *Dancehall Ladies: Executed Women of the 20th Century*, published by University Press of America, Lanham, MD, 2000.

26. *Ogden Standard-Examiner,* July 17, 1936, p. 1.
27. Howard Engel, *Lord High Executioner: An Unashamed Look at Hangmen, Headsmen, and Their Kind.* London: Firefly Books, 1996, p. 203.
28. *Tulsa Tribune,* December 18, 1953, p. 1.
29. Justin Atholl, *Shadow of the Gallows.* London: John Long Limited, 1954, p. 168.
30. Clinton T. Duffy, *88 Men and 2 Women.* Garden City, NY: Doubleday & Co., 1962, p. 141.

CHAPTER 3   PROCESS QUESTIONS

1. Fyodor Dostoevsky, *The Idiot.* New York: Bantam Books, 1958, pp. 20–21.
2. Clinton T. Duffy, *88 Men and Two Women.* Garden City, NY: Doubleday & Co., 1962, p. 135.
3. George Ryley Scott, *The History of Capital Punishment: Including an Examination of the Case For and Against the Death Penalty.* London: Torchstream Books, 1950, pp. 153–155.
4. Geoffrey Abbott, *The Book of Execution: An Encyclopedia of Methods of Judicial Execution.* London: Headline Book Publishing, 1994.
5. Ibid., p. 27.
6. Ibid., p. 307.
7. Ibid., p. 335.
8. Ibid., p. 89.
9. Ibid., p. 308.
10. Brian Bailey, *Hangmen of England: A History of Executions from Jack Ketch to Albert Pierrepoint.* London: W. H. Allen & Co., 1989, p. 193.
11. Albert Pierrepoint, *Executioner: Pierrepoint. The Amazing Autobiography of the World's Most Famous Executioner.* London: George G. Harrap & Co. Limited, 1974, p. 169.
12. Ibid., p. 176.
13. Ibid.
14. Syd Dernley with David Newman, *A Hangman's Tale: Memoirs of a Public Executioner.* London: Pan Books, 1990, p. 196.
15. Pierrepoint, p. 182.
16. Ibid., p. 92.
17. Arthur Koestler, *Reflections on Hanging.* New York: The Macmillan Company, 1957, p. 140.
18. Pierrepoint, p. 92.
19. *Cheyenne Daily Leader,* April 22, 1892.
20. *Wilkerson v. Utah,* October 1878.
21. Unpublished autobiography is in the author's possession.
22. *New York Times,* February 9, 1913, Section III, p. 2.
23. *Reno Evening Gazette,* May 14, 1913, p. 1.
24. *New York Tribune,* November 20, 1915.
25. Interview by Dan Rather for *60 Minutes* with Bob Holstein, member of the James Rodgers's firing squad, March 30, 1960.
26. Leonard A. Stevens, *Death Penalty.* New York: Coward, McCann & Geoghegan, Inc., 1978, p. 120.

27. Arnold Beichman, "The First Electrocution," *Commentary Magazine*, May 1963, p. 411.

28. Ibid., p. 414.

29. "Convicted Killer: Volunteers Offer to Pull the Switch," *Ogden Standard-Examiner*, April 28, 1980.

30. *The Salt Lake City Tribune*, July 11, 1936, p. 1.

31. *Carson City Daily Appeal*, March 19, 1921, p. 1.

32. "Gas Kills Convict Almost Instantly," *New York Times*, February 9, 1924, p. 15.

33. Ibid.

34. *New York Times*, April 13, 1925. Editorial.

35. Lou Jones, *Final Exposure: Portraits from Death Row*. Boston: Northeastern University Press, 1996, p. 76.

36. Phil Donahue interview, Transcript #10314, pp. 1–2.

37. Ibid., p. 2.

38. www.doc.state.nc.us/dop/deathpenalty/execution.htm.

39. James W. Marquart, Sheldon Ekland-Olson, and Jonathan R. Sorenson, *The Rope, the Chair, and the Needle: Capital Punishment in Texas, 1923–1990*. Austin: University of Texas, 1994, p. 133.

40. Ibid.

41. *Salt Lake Herald-Republican*, November 19, 1915.

42. Ibid.

43. *Industrial Worker*, December 2, 1916.

44. *Ogden Standard-Examiner*, December 9, 1988, p. 1A.

45. Ed Baumann, *May God Have Mercy on Your Soul: The Story of the Rope and the Thunderbolt*. Chicago: Bonus Books, Inc., 1993, p. 188.

46. Ibid., p. 189.

47. Ibid., p. 194.

48. Ibid., p. 197.

49. Ibid., p. 199.

50. *New York Times*, January 15, 1928, p. 20.

51. V. A. C. Gatrell, *The Hanging Tree: Execution and the English People, 1770–1868*. London: Oxford University Press, 1996, p. 33.

52. *Ogden Standard-Examiner*, February 11, 1996, p. 2.

53. *Ogden Standard-Examiner*, December 19, 1996, p. 5A.

54. *Ogden Standard-Examiner*, February 2, 1992, p. 8A.

55. *USA Today*, June 11, 2001, p. 13A.

56. Ibid.

57. Robert Christophe, *The Executioners*. New York: Ace Books, Inc., 1961, p. 29.

58. Ibid.

59. Ibid., p. 11.

60. Ibid., p. 8.

61. Ibid., p. 68.

62. Ibid., p. 75.

63. Bailey, p. 11.

64. Ibid.

65. Howard Engel, *Lord High Executioner: An Unashamed Look at Hangmen, Headsmen, and Their Kind*. Buffalo, NY: Firefly Books, Inc., 1966, pp. 71, 86.

66. Ibid., p. 50.

67. Bailey, p. 103.

68. Engel, p. 171.
69. Bailey, p. 140.
70. John D. Bessler, *Death in the Dark: Midnight Executions in America.* Boston: Northeastern University Press, 1997, p. 150.
71. Engel, p. 69.
72. Syd Dernley with David Newman, *The Hangman's Tale: Memoirs of a Public Executioner.* London: Pan Books, 1990, p. 196.
73. Bailey, p. 110.
74. Dernley, p. 199.
75. Ibid., p. 200.
76. Pierrepoint, p. 34.
77. Ibid., p. 10.
78. Justin Atholl, *Reluctant Hangman: The Story of James Berry, Executioner 1884–1892.* London: John Long Limited, 1956, p. 71.
79. Ibid., pp. 72–73.
80. Egyptian state executioner Helmi Sultan. *Newsweek,* September 9, 1991, p. 17.
81. Robert Elliott with Albert R. Beatty, *Agent of Death: The Memoirs of an Executioner.* New York: E. P. Dutton, Co., 1940, p. 240.
82. Ibid., p. 15.
83. Ibid., p. 149.
84. Ibid., pp. 145–146.
85. Ibid., pp. 302–303.
86. Engel, p. 75.
87. Pierrepoint, p. 125.
88. Ibid., p. 76.
89. Elliott, pp. 299–301.
90. *USA Today,* February, 2, 2001, p. 6A.
91. Statement by Governor Toney Anaya on Crime and Capital Punishment. Santa Fe, New Mexico, November 26, 1986.
92. *LIFElines,* January–March, No. 51, 1992, p. 1.
93. *The Saturday Evening Post,* March 22, 1958, p. 82.
94. Ibid., p. 84.
95. Ibid.
96. Winthrop Rockefeller, "Executive Clemency and the Death Penalty," *Catholic University Law Review,* 21:94, pp. 1–2.
97. Federal Bureau of Prisons, "Legal Eagle of August," 2001, pp. 4–5.
98. Jerry Harkavy, "Few Details Remain of First Man to Face Federal Execution," *Las Vegas Review Journal,* June 10, 2001, p. 4B.
99. Watt Espy and John Ortiz, "Executions in the U.S. 1608–1987: The Espy File," Inter-University Consortium for Political and Social Research, 1994.
100. Lloyd Lewis, *The Assassination of Lincoln: History and Myth.* Lincoln: University of Nebraska, 1994.
101. *San Francisco Chronicle,* October 18, 1895, p. 8.
102. Robert and Michael Meeropol, *We Are Your Sons: The Legacy of Ethel and Julius Rosenberg.* New York: Ballantine Books, 1975, p. 262.
103. Sam Robert, *The Brother.* New York: Random House.
104. *Las Vegas Review-Journal,* December 6, 2001, p. 15A.
105. Ibid.

CHAPTER 4   CURRENT ISSUES QUESTIONS

1. Amnesty International—USA Program to Abolish the Death Penalty.
2. *USA Today*, July 10, 1997, p. 4A.
3. Mark Costanzo, *Just Revenge: Costs and Consequences of the Death Penalty*. New York: St. Martin's Press, 1997, p. 63.
4. 208.55.30.156/facts/other/costly.shtml.
5. Margaret Radin, "Cruel Punishment and Respect for Persons: Super Due Process for Death," *Southern California Law Review*, 53:1143–1185.
6. 208.55.30.156/facts/other/costly.shtml.
7. Wysiwyg://13/htpp://www.geocities.com/Area51/Capsule/2698/cp.html, p. 13.
8. Robert M. Bohm, *Deathquest: Introduction to the Theory and Practice of Capital Punishment in the United States*. Cincinnati, OH: Anderson Publishing, 1999, p. 116.
9. Ibid., p. 109.
10. Costanzo, p. 64.
11. Arthur Koestler, *Reflections on Hanging*. New York: Macmillan Co., 1957, p. 13.
12. *The Tennessean*, October 16, 1985, p. 1.
13. Victor Streib, "The Juvenile Death Penalty Today: Death Sentences and Executions for Juvenile Crimes, January 1973–May 1998," pp. 11–17.
14. *Deseret News*, February 2, 1987, p. 3.
15. *Ogden Standard-Examiner*, June 27, 1989, p. 3A.
16. My notes, May 18, 1989.
17. *Criminal Justice Newsletter*, January 2000, 30:17, p. 1.
18. Ibid.
19. *Ogden Standard-Examiner*, June 12, 2000, p. A1.
20. Case of Leonel Torres Herrera reported in www.lightworks.com/MonthlyAspectarian/1996/March/17-0396.html, p. 3.
21. Michael Radelet, Hugo Bedau, and Constance Putnam, *In Spite of Innocence: Erroneous Convictions in Capital Cases*. Boston: Northeastern University Press, 1992.
22. Ibid., pp. 16–17.
23. Ibid., pp. 272–273.
24. Gillespie, 2000, pp. 37–38.
25. Ludovic Kennedy, *The Airman and the Carpenter*. New York: Viking Penguin, Inc., 1985, p. 255.
26. *Ogden Standard-Examiner*, October 23, 1994, p. 5E.
27. Robert H. Montgomery, *Sacco-Vanzetti: The Murder and the Myth*. New York: Devin-Adair Co., 1960, p. 59.
28. W. G. Thompson, *The Atlantic Monthly*, February 1928, as quoted in *The Letters of Sacco and Vanzetti*. Marion D. Frankfurter and Gardner Jackson, eds. New York: E. P. Dutton & Co., 1950.
29. From a proclamation by Governor Michael S. Dukakis signed July 19, 1977.
30. Ibid.
31. Radelet et al., p. 314.
32. Copy of letter in my file provided by Folke G. Anderson, April 8, 1979.
33. www.deathpenaltyinfo.org/innocothers.html.
34. Ibid.

35. Ibid.
36. *The Washington Post*, February 17, 1999, p. C1.
37. *USA Today*, July 19, 2001, p. 3A.
38. *Newsweek*, August 28, 1989, p. 15.

CHAPTER 5   CONCLUSION: WHAT HAVE I LEARNED?

1. *Columbus Evening Dispatch*, December 8, 1938, p. 8–B.
2. Wenzel Brown, *The Lonely Hearts Murderers*. New York: Greenberg Publishers, 1952, p. 115.